CHARLES A. LINDBERGH
A PHOTOGRAPHIC ALBUM

JOSHUA STOFF

DOVER PUBLICATIONS, INC.
New York

Copyright

Copyright © 1995 by Joshua Stoff.
All rights reserved under Pan American and International Copyright Conventions.

Published in Canada by General Publishing Company, Ltd., 30 Lesmill Road, Don Mills, Toronto, Ontario.
Published in the United Kingdom by Constable and Company, Ltd., 3 The Lanchesters, 162-164 Fulham Palace Road, London W6 9ER.

Bibliographical Note

Charles A. Lindbergh: A Photographic Album is a new work, first published by Dover Publications, Inc., in 1995.

Edited by Alan Weissman

Designed by Jeanne Joudry

An index appears on pages 163-165.

Library of Congress Cataloging-in-Publication Data

Stoff, Joshua.
    Charles A. Lindbergh : a photographic album / Joshua Stoff.
       p.   cm.
    Includes index.
    ISBN 0-486-27878-6 (pbk.)
    1. Lindbergh, Charles A. (Charles Augustus), 1902-1974—Portraits.
2. Air pilots—United States—Biography. I. Title.
TL540.L5S76   1995
629.13'092—dc20   94-12121
[B]   CIP

Manufactured in the United States of America
Dover Publications, Inc., 31 East 2nd Street, Mineola, N.Y. 11501

Introduction

Almost literally overnight, Charles A. Lindbergh was transformed from an obscure airmail pilot into the most famous aviator in the world. At the age of 25, he had accomplished what no man had done before, having flown nonstop from New York to Paris, 3,600 miles across the cold waters of the Atlantic. Moreover, he did it alone, in a small single-engine monoplane. The danger and daring of such a feat are highlighted by the fact that to this day no one else has flown alone, nonstop, from New York to Paris in a single-engine plane. Not only did this accomplishment make Lindbergh a hero and one of the most lionized personalities in the world for decades, it popularized, even revolutionized aviation like no other single event before or since, with the possible exception of the pioneering flight of the Wright brothers. Now, more than 65 years later, Lindbergh's achievement—as well as other events in his life, at least one of them tragic—justly continues to receive attention in new books and articles added to the stream of writings that have made him one of the most studied and celebrated heroes in American history.

Lindbergh's grandfather, August Lindbergh, was a lawyer and a reform member of the Swedish parliament who emigrated to Minnesota when Charles's father was an infant. Charles's father, Charles August Lindbergh, Sr. (distinguished here as "Sr." from his son—"Jr."—though their names were not precisely the same), also became a lawyer and in 1884 established a practice in Little Falls, Minnesota, living on a 120-acre farm there. In 1901 he married a local schoolteacher, Miss Evangeline Lodge Land. On February 4, 1902, Charles Augustus Lindbergh, Jr., was born in his maternal grandparents' house in Detroit. Two months later, he was taken to Little Falls.

Charles's maternal grandfather, Dr. (so called though he had never formally taken a degree) Charles H. Land, a pioneer dentist, scientist and inventor, was a major formative influence on his young grandson. Lindbergh's mother, with a degree in chemistry from the University of Michigan, was exceptionally well educated for a woman of her day, and she further encouraged her son's interest in science. Outings with his father sparked a love in young Charles for the robust outdoor life. In Minnesota, encouraged to be self-sufficient, Charles was taught to shoot at age six, though he could hardly lift his rifle. At age eleven Charles was taught to drive and became fascinated by the inner working of automobiles. During his childhood he was enrolled in eleven different schools, but he altogether disliked every one of them. Always a loner, he preferred to pursue his favorite studies on his own.

Charles Lindbergh, Sr., a Roosevelt Republican with a radical, reformist bent, became deeply committed to social reform and was elected to Congress in 1906. Thereafter the family spent much of the year in Washington, D.C. When war broke out in Europe, Congressman Lindbergh, critical of the political influence of big business, opposed American entry into World War I, which he saw as a connivance solely in the interests of the giant corporate trusts and Wall Street financial institutions. His father's political position undoubtedly had a heavy influence on Charles Junior's later thinking.

During his last two years in Little Falls, Charles ran his father's farm, and then in 1920 he entered the University of Wisconsin at Madison to study engineering. Less than two years later, he gave up school to learn to fly.

Lindbergh decided upon a career in aviation because flying seemed an ideal combination of his interests in science and the outdoors. After receiving informal flying instruction in Nebraska in 1922, he performed for a time with a Midwestern barnstorming troupe. In 1923, with financial assistance from his father, Charles purchased his first airplane, a World War I surplus Curtiss JN-4 "Jenny." For a while he barnstormed alone in his Jenny, but then, tired of its limitations and yearning to fly newer, more advanced aircraft, he joined the Army Air Service, which offered the only opportunity to do this.

At training fields in Texas in 1924 and 1925, flying Cadet Lindbergh found that without qualifying grades he could not pass the tests to become a commissioned pilot. For the first time he realized the importance of hard study in achieving his goals, and the formerly indifferent student now aimed at perfection, became a dedicated scholar and graduated first in his class. In March 1925 he was commissioned a Second Lieutenant in the Army Reserve. On the way to this goal he had had considerable practical flying experience as well, sometimes risking his life, as when he made a narrow escape by parachute in a midair collision. In June he made a second emergency parachute jump after a civil airplane he was testing refused to come out of a spin.

After several months of instructing in the St. Louis area, Lindbergh was appointed chief pilot of the Robertson Aircraft Corporation, leading to his initiating the first airmail flight between St. Louis and Chicago in April 1926. Thereafter, Lindbergh regularly flew this mail run in a De Havilland DH-4.

Lack of proper instrumentation, landing fields, lighting devices and accurate weather forecasts all made flying the mail extremely dangerous at this time. Twice Lindbergh was forced to make emergency parachute jumps after running out of fuel at night in poor weather.

At least a pilot had time to himself. It was during the lonely hours flying the mail at night that Lindbergh conceived the idea of competing for the Orteig Prize of $25,000, offered in 1919 for the first nonstop flight between Paris and New York. Lindbergh was intrigued by the idea of publicly demonstrating how the airplane could safely link the New World with the Old, at the same time giving the civilian pilot enhanced credibility. Winning the money was not his prime objective; the Orteig Prize would barely cover the cost of the plane, the fuel and all necessary equipment. As for the danger, Lindbergh could not imagine the weather being worse or the flight more dangerous than what he had already experienced flying the mail.

Not luck, as claimed by the press, but experience and expert planning insured the success of Lindbergh's flight. Every detail was carefully thought out. He decided upon a single-engine plane because it would have greater range than a multiengine plane and could be more streamlined, as the engine would be in the nose. Furthermore, Lindbergh felt that a multiengine plane would be no safer anyway because it couldn't fly for very long after even one of its three engines had stopped.

At the time the best planes available of the type needed were made by Bellanca. Lindbergh had been turned down in his attempt to buy one, however, so, instead, with the backing of eight St. Louis businessmen, he ordered, from the Ryan Aircraft Corporation of San Diego, a specially designed aircraft to be custom-built in two months. The Ryan "NYP" (for "New York to Paris"), a high-wing monoplane, was a variation of one of Ryan's reliable mail planes. An enormous fuel tank was installed, blocking the pilot's forward vision, and power was provided by the Wright J-5 "Whirlwind," one of the most reliable engines of the day. Given the technology of the time, this was the best possible plane for the task at hand.

Having concluded flight testing by early May 1927, Lindbergh flew his plane, now called the *Spirit of St. Louis* (in appreciation of the funding by the businessmen from that city), from San Diego to St. Louis and on to Curtiss Field, Long Island, about twenty miles east of the center of New York City. Lindbergh attracted a great deal of attention in New York, partly because he had made the cross-country flight in record time. There were other reasons as well. Lindbergh was young and of an "all-American" type, although he was also a quiet loner. Of the three major trans-Atlantic competitors, he was the only one who planned to attempt the crossing alone.

For a while, conditions were not right. Lindbergh spent several days tuning his plane, knocking about the New York area, and waiting at the Garden City Hotel for the weather to clear. He had stored his Ryan at Curtiss Field, but on the rainy morning of May 20 he had it moved east to neighboring Roosevelt Field, which had a longer runway. Weighing his chances, Lindbergh had decided that this was his moment.

At 7:52 A.M., Lindbergh headed his silver monoplane eastward down the muddy mile-long runway, heavily loaded with 2,750 pounds of fuel (slightly more than the aircraft had been designed to take off with). At liftoff, he barely cleared the trees at the end of the runway.

Once Lindbergh was aloft, the entire country prayed for him. Many stood transfixed by their radios as they listened for news of his journey. The "Lone Eagle" was heading into the unknown.

After a flight of 33 hours and 30 minutes, in which he stubbornly fought off drowsiness and was called upon to exercise his remarkable navigational skills, the exhausted Lindbergh arrived triumphantly in Paris.

More than any other single flight since the Wright brothers, Lindbergh's triumph revolutionized aviation. For one thing, from a technological standpoint, his timing couldn't have been better. Lindbergh made his crossing at a time when more reliable aircraft engines with better power-to-weight ratios, as well as improved navigational devices, had begun to bring long-range flying reasonably within reach of the average citizen.

Moreover, the style of Lindbergh's achievement appealed greatly to the public. It enhanced the credibility of the civilian pilot and demonstrated the enormous potential of aviation. Although the *Spirit of St. Louis* was itself of no possible use as an airliner, it stimulated the public's imagination. People began to give serious thought to traveling by air, and this soon led to the explosive development of the American aircraft industry.

Previously, only the military and sport values of aviation had been demonstrated. Even the airmail system had been little utilized. In the year following Lindbergh's flight, however, the number of passengers carried on commercial airliners quadrupled as public confidence in them soared. This marked the real beginning of commercial aviation. Lindbergh had foreseen this when he wrote, earlier in 1927, "The year will surely come when passengers and mail will fly every day from America to Europe."

Following his epoch-making flight, his return to New York and a week of celebrations there and in Washington, Lindbergh went to St. Louis to thank his backers. All the while he was contemplating his future role in the development of aviation. He saw himself now less as a pioneer than as a missionary bringing the gospel of aviation to the people of America. He had personally demonstrated what the airplane was capable of. Now he had to incite the public to provide municipal airfields and whatever else was necessary to support commercial aviation. Then, starting in July 1927, Lindbergh began a 22,000-mile tour of the United States on behalf of the Guggenheim Fund for the Promotion of Aeronautics. This three-month tour demonstrated with clockwork precision that airplanes could now safely fly to specific places at predetermined times. Next, President Calles of Mexico invited Lindbergh on an official visit. He responded on December 13 by flying nonstop from Washington to Mexico City in 27 hours, 15 minutes. From there he headed south on a 9,000-mile goodwill tour of Latin America, and finally, in April 1928, he delivered the *Spirit of St. Louis* to the Smithsonian Institution, where it still hangs today.

After this, working as a consultant for several companies, Lindbergh surveyed air routes and promoted airport development. As Technical Committee Chairman for Transcontinental Air Transport (TAT), he helped develop the first transcontinental airline service, which began in 1929. The line soon became TWA, which, like TAT, was known as "The Lindbergh Line." Lindbergh also worked as a consultant for Pan American Airways and set up the earliest Caribbean airline routes. Through all this, although he yearned for a quiet life, Lindbergh remained the target of intense media publicity.

In May 1929, Lindbergh married Anne Morrow, daughter of the American Ambassador to Mexico, whom he had met on his 1927 flight there. Later in 1929 Anne assisted her husband in yet more work for both TAT and Pan Am, and they worked together on archaeological survey flights to discover Mayan ruins. Throughout, Lindbergh remained an object of unprecedented public adulation.

In 1929, Lindbergh heard of the pioneering rocketry experiments of Dr. Robert Goddard. Believing that rocket propulsion would have a great deal to do with the future of aviation, Lindbergh became very interested in Goddard's work and he obtained financial assistance for him from the Carnegie Institution and from the father of his millionaire friend Harry Guggenheim. By the mid-1930's, in New Mexico, he was able to see the first hesitant steps into rocket-propelled flight that would one day carry humans to the moon.

In June 1930 a son, Charles Lindbergh, Jr., was born. As

always, the news media used the occasion to churn up a sea of publicity. At this time Lindbergh continued to act as a consultant for TAT and Pan Am. He also began a new phase of his life after he and Anne had moved into a country home not far from Princeton, N.J. At Princeton University, he became interested in the work of the controversial scientist Dr. Alexis Carrel, who at this time was trying to perfect the "perfusion pump," a predecessor of the modern artificial heart. Over the next few years, when not on survey flights, Lindbergh spent much time working in Carrel's laboratory. The pioneering aviator proved also to be a highly competent scientist, and made significant contributions. Later, Lindbergh, alone or in collaboration with Carrel, wrote several articles on their work, which were published in various scientific journals. He also collaborated with Carrel on a book describing their work, *The Culture of Organs*, published in 1938.

In 1930 Lindbergh also ordered a specially built monoplane, a Lockheed "Sirius." Upon its completion, Charles and Anne flew it from Los Angeles to New York, setting a new transcontinental speed record. In New York it was fitted with EDO floats in place of wheels, and with state-of-the-art radio and emergency equipment, making it without doubt the most advanced seaplane in the world at that time.

Beginning on July 27, 1931, this specially improved Sirius was used by the Lindberghs for a long survey flight by the Great Circle route over northern Canada, Alaska and Siberia, and then down to Japan and China, where they departed from their original plans to assist a famine-relief team from the Rockefeller Institute working in the Yangtze valley with victims of flooding. In October, in Hangkow, the Sirius was badly damaged as it was being lowered from the deck of an aircraft carrier where it was being stored, and the Lindberghs themselves, who were inside the plane, had a narrow escape. Although their 10,000-mile flight (clearly the longest ever made by a floatplane without preplanned assistance) had been cut short, they had still made valuable discoveries about seaplane harbors in remote areas where no airplane had ever landed before.

Then, on March 1, 1932, came a shock that changed the Lindberghs' lives forever. Their twenty-month-old son, Charles Jr., was kidnapped from their home in rural New Jersey. Two months later the child's corpse was discovered in the woods not far away. For most of this period the Lindberghs' time was occupied by the hunt for the culprit. Naturally, the news media pounced on the affair and soon the world knew of the tragedy, which became one of the most notorious crimes in history. Though Lindbergh had always had an antagonistic relationship with the press, at first he swallowed his pride and enlisted their help. When one of the tabloids published an unauthorized picture of the child's mangled corpse, however, this reinforced his conviction that the press was fundamentally irresponsible, and for some time, with occasional carefully chosen exceptions, he refused to have anything to do with journalists.

In August 1932, Anne gave birth to another son, Jon. Then, in desperate need for distraction from painful memories (and assured that the search for their son's killer was still being pursued vigorously by the authorities), the following year they made another survey flight in their Lockheed Sirius floatplane, this time over the North—and later the South—Atlantic Ocean. Like many previous survey flights, this one was partly sponsored by Pan American Airways to obtain information about potential seaplane harbors for future air routes.

Once again they followed a Great Circle route, this time through Newfoundland, Labrador, Greenland, Iceland and the Faeroe Islands. In Greenland, where they spent three weeks, an Eskimo boy named their plane *Tingmissartoq*, which means "one who flies like a big bird." Crossing to Europe, they visited several major cities, including Moscow, and eventually made their way home over the South Atlantic, flying to Brazil, Trinidad and Puerto Rico before landing again at the seaplane dock in College Point, New York. The 30,000-mile flight, greater than the circumference of the earth, set yet another record.

On their return, the Lindberghs were once again faced with the circumstances surrounding the unsolved murder of their son. In a long-drawn-out, complicated affair, Bruno Richard Hauptmann, an unemployed German immigrant with a criminal record in his homeland, was arrested in 1934, convicted in 1935 and executed in 1936. It was never discovered whether he had any accomplices. To this day books continue to appear questioning not only this fact but practically every other in the case, including that of Hauptmann's guilt.

In 1934 another unpleasant incident revolved around Lindbergh's questioning President Roosevelt's cancellation of all private airmail contracts. Continued bitterness between Lindbergh and Roosevelt led to the former's resignation of his commission in the Army Air Corps Reserve, in 1941.

After the kidnapping case was settled, living in the United States was so painful to the Lindberghs that they spent several years in Europe, residing primarily in Great Britain but flying all over Europe and even Asia. In mid-1936, Lindbergh also made the first of a number of visits to Germany as the guest of the Nazi government. Although the visits were made with the support of the American authorities and Lindbergh in fact dutifully reported on many technical details of German airplanes, these visits later came back to haunt him. Lindbergh was convinced of the superiority of German air power, was the recipient of a medal awarded by the Nazis, and had made some statements critical of American society and praising the values of the German people. Later, when war threatened in Europe, Lindbergh was also rigidly opposed to American participation (as his father had been opposed to our entering the First World War two decades before). Lindbergh's situation and his openly expressed antiwar views only worsened the antagonism between him and President Roosevelt, and his failure to make any public explanation of his views to the press, which he continued to loathe, led to the growth of the belief by the public that he was a Nazi sympathizer. He was not to rid himself of this stigma for years.

In 1938 the Lindberghs moved to the Continent, living for a time in a stone manor house on a tiny island off the coast of Brittany, where the conditions were primitive. They had planned to move to Berlin in the fall, but changed their minds at signs of increasing Nazi violence.

By the time World War II had broken out in Europe, the Lindberghs were safely back in the United States and living on Long Island. At first Lindbergh was involved in civil and military aeronautics. Then came an uncharacteristic lapse in his break with the news media when he made a nationwide radio address. In that and subsequent addresses he presented views that were uncompromisingly against American intervention in the European war and even against aid to Britain, leading to an estrangement from the President and the public, and in 1941 to the resignation of his Air Corps commission.

After Pearl Harbor at the end of that year, however, seeing that America was in fact going to war, Lindbergh sought, unsuccessfully, to have his commission reinstated. Now eager to assist the war effort, at first he helped Henry

Ford build airplanes in Detroit. In 1944, he managed to get himself appointed a "civilian observer" in the Pacific, flying a Chance-Vought F-4U "Corsair." With the secret help of friends in the military, he was soon flying in combat missions against the Japanese. Ultimately he participated in fifty of these, escorting bombers and attacking ground targets. Once he shot down a Japanese fighter; another time, he was nearly shot down himself. On other occasions he flew a Lockheed P-38 "Lightning." To the amazement of Air Corps officers, he was able to operate the plane using one-third less fuel than any pilot in the elite 475th Fighter Group. This led to his most valuable wartime work, instructing military pilots in fuel economy.

After V-E Day in 1945, Lindbergh went to Germany to help recruit German scientists for American research projects. For the next decade he was involved as a technical consultant on a number of projects to develop advanced air power, both civilian and military (by now he was convinced of the futility of his old antiwar, isolationist views, given the danger posed to the free world by the existence of powerful bombers and rockets). His civilian work was, once again, for Pan American, and much of it concerned the development of the jet airliners that came to dominate commercial flying and are now commonplace.

Finally, official recognition of Lindbergh's military contributions came in 1954 when President Eisenhower restored his commission in the Air Force Reserve and promoted him to Brigadier General.

In 1953 Lindbergh published an account of his most famous flight, named, after the plane, *The Spirit of St. Louis*. It was highly acclaimed, winning a Pulitzer Prize and becoming a best-seller. In 1957 it was made into a feature film starring James Stewart.

Lindbergh's activities in the 1960's were highly diverse. As always, he was a valued consultant on aircraft and aviation. He also again took up the work on the perfusion pump that he had done with Dr. Alexis Carrel thirty years before. Working with Dr. Theodore Malinin of the Naval Research Institute in Bethesda, Maryland, he came up with a working model based on newer technology. In a version manufactured by Corning Glass, it was actually used by researchers.

One of Lindbergh's more unusual experiences in the 1960's was his living for a time with the Masai people of Kenya in Africa. In the middle of the decade he also became heavily involved in conservation activities with the World Wildlife Fund, continuing until nearly the end of his life. He also did a great deal of work in support of oppressed minorities in the Philippines.

In 1972 Lindbergh discovered he had cancer. By 1974 the disease had progressed so far that he knew his days were numbered. He had himself flown from Columbia Presbyterian Hospital in New York to Maui, where the Lindberghs had maintained a winter home. This was his favorite spot on earth. In his last days he planned his burial with the care he had formerly devoted to a long-range flight. He died peacefully on August 26, 1974. Inscribed on his tomb are these words from the 139th Psalm:

". . . If I take the wings of the morning, and dwell in the uttermost parts of the sea . . ."

Of Charles Lindbergh's many achievements, the best remembered will always be his historic flight to Paris in 1927. In those few hours, his dedication, courage, understanding and wisdom opened the eyes of the world to the possibilities of aviation and made his name that of one of the great pioneers of all time.

CHARLES A. LINDBERGH
A PHOTOGRAPHIC ALBUM

1. Not trusting the local Swedish midwives in Little Falls, Minnesota, Evangeline Land Lindbergh returned to her parents' home in Detroit to have her baby. Thus, Charles Lindbergh was born in Detroit on February 4, 1902. Here he is learning to walk at the age of fourteen months.

2. Charles's mother, born Evangeline Lodge Land, was a high-school science teacher in Little Falls, Minnesota, when she met Charles Lindbergh, Sr., a locally prominent lawyer. They were married in March 1901. Thus it was that Charles Jr. came to grow up in rural Minnesota, near the headwaters of the Mississippi River. He is seen here about 1908. *(Photo: Yale University Library.)*

1

2

3. Charles Lindbergh, Sr., born in Stockholm, Sweden, had emigrated to the United States as an infant. He became a lawyer and then, after increasing involvement in politics, was elected to Congress in 1906. His isolationist views during World War I certainly influenced his son's thinking during the early years of World War II. He is seen here with eight-year-old Charles Lindbergh, Jr., about 1910. *(Photo: Cradle of Aviation Museum, Mitchel Field, Garden City, New York.)*

4. While his family was living in Washington in 1912, young Charles saw an air show at nearby Fort Myer, Virginia. Seeing airplanes like this Wright biplane flying, racing and bombing left an impression on Lindbergh that would alter the course of his life. He had always been interested in mechanical things. Combining this with his new fascination by what he saw as the freedom of flying, young Charles knew he had to be a flier himself someday. *(Photo: Cradle of Aviation Museum.)*

3

4

5

5. Lindbergh (center) in front of a Lincoln-Standard "Tour-about" while learning to fly in Nebraska, April 1922. Note the dog on the wing. Lindbergh did not solo here, because he lacked enough money to post a bond to cover possible damage to the airplane. *(Photo: National Air and Space Museum.)*

7

8

6. Lindbergh (left) and barnstorming friend "Bud" Gurney in front of a Standard J-1, about 1923. Lindbergh met Gurney at the Nebraska Aircraft School in 1922 and they later did parachute jumps and stunt flying together at fairs. They also flew together to the St. Louis Air Races in 1923. *(Photo: Missouri Historical Society.)*

7. "Slim" Lindbergh (center, kneeling), as he was known in this

period of his life, with barnstorming friends, about 1923. *(Photo: National Air and Space Museum.)*

8. In April 1923, Lindbergh purchased a war-surplus Curtiss JN-4 "Jenny" for five hundred dollars in Americus, Georgia. He briefly barnstormed the Southeast before heading north to Minnesota. When he purchased the plane, he had not yet soloed. Here are the results of an engine failure at Pensacola, Florida. *(Photo: Lindbergh House, Little Falls, Minnesota.)*

9

9. Lindbergh's plane, the JN-4, was the aircraft most typically used in the 1920's by the barnstormers, men who made a living by flying from town to town and taking people for rides. Despite its limited power and questionable stability, the Jenny was the mainstay of barnstorming. The average speed of the Jenny did not vary much between landing speed (60 mph) and flying speed (70 mph). Moreover, it had no brakes! Lindbergh and barnstorming friend Leon Klink can be seen in the cockpits, with perhaps a potential passenger posing by the wing. Note the bicycle wedged in the flying wires. *(Photo: Lindbergh House.)*

10. Like other barnstormers, Lindbergh usually tried to meet expenses, in part, by trading plane rides for room and board. On many nights, however, he was forced to sleep under the plane's wing. Here Lindbergh (right) and Klink pose in front of the tired Jenny somewhere in the Midwest. *(Photo: Cradle of Aviation Museum.)*

11

12

11. C. A. (as Charles Senior was usually called in the family) Lindbergh, at left, and Charles Junior assessing the damage to the Jenny on June 8, 1923. Charles had been flying his father, who was running for the U.S. Senate, to one of a number of campaign stops when the plane ran into a ditch on take-off from a farm near Glencoe, Minnesota. *(Photo: Cradle of Aviation Museum.)*

12. During a barnstorming trip, Lindbergh (right), sitting on the engine, fills the Jenny's tank with gas while Leon Klink looks at the camera. After barnstorming through Minnesota and Wisconsin in October 1923, Lindbergh flew the Jenny on a circuitous 1,200-mile path, barnstorming along the way, to St. Louis for the National Air Races. Afterward, he took on some students in Illinois. Finally, before the end of the year, he flew the Jenny to Iowa and sold it to one of Bud Gurney's friends. *(Photo: Lindbergh House.)*

13. Second Lt. Charles A. Lindbergh, Kelly Field, Texas, March 1925. Lindbergh had given up barnstorming in 1924, not because it was dangerous but because of its uncertain future. The occupation was overcrowded, and pilots could barely make a living. Realizing that he would need better credentials to get ahead in aviation, Lindbergh, after selling his Jenny, joined the U.S. Army Air Service, reporting for duty on March 15, 1924. He knew also that only in the military would he have the chance to fly the most advanced planes. *(Photo: National Air and Space Museum.)*

14. The Army sent Lindbergh to Brooks Field, Texas, where he trained on Jennys fitted, like the one in this photo, with powerful Hispano-Suiza engines. With over three hundred hours as a barnstormer under his belt he was soon, not surprisingly, flying circles around his classmates, most of whom had never flown before. *(Photo: National Air and Space Museum.)*

13

14

15. Flying for the Army was every bit as dangerous as barn-storming. On one occasion, flying an SE-5 fighter, like the one shown here, Lindbergh was involved in a midair collision with another plane during a mock dogfight. Lindbergh and the other pilot were lucky to survive—theirs was the first class to be issued parachutes. The SE-5 Lindbergh flew in the Army had been one of the leading British fighters of World War I. After the war, Curtiss assembled some more fighters of this type to serve as advanced trainers. Others that had actually been used in the war were sent home with U.S. squadrons after the Armistice. SE-5's continued to be used as advanced trainers until 1927. *(Photo: Cradle of Aviation Museum.)*

16. Wanting to stay involved with military aviation, in the summer of 1925 Lindbergh joined a Missouri National Guard Squadron based at Lambert Field, St. Louis. As the peacetime Army was short of funds, Lindbergh was released from duty after receiving his wings. Thus, his stint as an Army test pilot was brief. Here he is after a parachute escape from a spinning experimental plane that had been known as the "Plywood Special," Lambert Field, June 2, 1925. Lindbergh landed in a strong wind and dislocated his shoulder. Note the wreckage in the background. *(Photo: National Air and Space Museum.)*

16

15

17

18

17. In 1926, after having barnstormed again for a while, Lindbergh signed on as Chief Pilot for the Robertson Aircraft Corporation in St. Louis. His assignment was to lay out and fly the new 285-mile airmail route between St. Louis and Chicago, choosing emergency landing fields and arranging fuel supplies. The Robertson brothers, who owned the company, could not afford beacons or radios; the only field lights were lanterns set by the side of the field. The main hazard in flying the mail came from the regularity it demanded. The mail had to get through regardless of weather, exposing airmail pilots to especially dangerous situations. As a result, 31 of the first 40 airmail pilots were killed. *(Photo: National Air and Space Museum.)*

18. Lindbergh inaugurated his airmail career at 5:30 A.M., April 15, 1926. Here, for the first run from St. Louis to Chicago, he loads the first sack of mail onto one of Robertson's De Havilland DH-4's. The war-surplus DH-4's then in use were powered by 400-hp Liberty engines. Top speed was 120 mph.

As Army salvage aircraft, the DH-4's had, according to Lindbergh, "rotting longerons, rusting wires and fittings, badly torn fabric, etc." When none of this interfered, the run from St. Louis to Chicago generally took three hours. *(Photo: Glen Apfelbaum Collection.)*

19. The same plane as in the previous photo—in slightly different circumstances! Lindbergh stands fourth from left, wearing high boots. This crash occurred when he ran out of fuel while trying to locate the airport in a heavy fog near Chicago on the night of September 15, 1926. No one had told him that his 120-gallon gasoline tank had been replaced by one holding only 80 gallons! With incidents like this, it is not surprising that Lindbergh had accepted his Chief Pilot's job with Robertson only "with the understanding that each pilot be furnished with a new seat-type silk parachute and that no criticism be made if the parachutes were used." *(Photo: Lindbergh House.)*

20

21

22

20. The remains of Lindbergh's DH-4 after his second bailout, on November 4, 1926. He had been unable to see the ground in a storm; later he found that his only field-illuminating flare had failed. *(Photo: Cradle of Aviation Museum.)*

21. St. Louis, date unknown. Lindbergh is at the controls while mailbags are being loaded for a flight to Chicago. The man standing at the far right is owner Frank Robertson. *(Photo: Cradle of Aviation Museum.)*

22. Lindbergh in the rear cockpit of a Robertson mail plane. It was on a lonely night run to Chicago that he conceived the great idea of making a nonstop flight to Paris. New, more reliable engines were now available, and what could be more dangerous than what he was doing now? *(Photo: Cradle of Aviation Museum.)*

23. Raymond Orteig, wealthy New York hotel owner of French ancestry, who on May 19, 1919, offered a prize of $25,000 for the first aviator to fly nonstop from New York to Paris. In 1919, however, the airplane did not exist that was technically advanced enough to accomplish this. *(Photo: Cradle of Aviation Museum.)*

23

24

24. Curtiss Field, Long Island, New York, about 1927. The largest airfield in the United States for the private flier, this became the home base of trans-Atlantic fliers during the "summer of eagles" in 1927. The *Spirit of St. Louis* was kept in a hangar just to the left of those shown in this photo ("Hangar Row"). It was towed past Hangar Row to Roosevelt Field on the morning of May 20, 1927. *(Photo: Cradle of Aviation Museum.)*

25. The entrance to Curtiss Field, ca. 1927. The Sikorsky hangar in the rear is where the ill-fated S-35 (see photo 27) was built. *(Photo: Cradle of Aviation Museum.)*

26

26. Aerial view of Roosevelt and Curtiss Fields, ca. 1931. Curtiss
Field extends from the lower-right through the mid-upper-
left portions of the photo. The *Spirit of St. Louis* was placed
in Hangar 16, the last hangar at the lower right. Roosevelt
Field begins at the upper left center, adjacent to Curtiss Field
and separated from it by a small hill and gully, the sandy area
running horizontally through the middle of the photo.
Lindbergh took off from a dirt runway that can still be seen in
this photo (right of center), although by this time it had been
bisected by a polo field. *(Photo: Cradle of Aviation Museum.)*

27. In 1926, famous French war ace René Fonck announced that
he would compete for the Orteig Prize, and set up a base at
Roosevelt Field. Fonck had a Sikorsky S-35 specially built
with three borrowed French engines. Wanting to make the
trip in style, the flamboyant Fonck hired an interior decora-
tor to install carpets, draperies, a refrigerator and a red
leather couch. Unfortunately, excess weight had been a problem from the start, and all these furnishings made the load on
each square foot of the Sikorsky's wings 26 pounds, where
they had been designed to carry only 19. This picture was
taken during a test flight over Roosevelt Field. *(Photo:
Cradle of Aviation Museum.)*

27

28

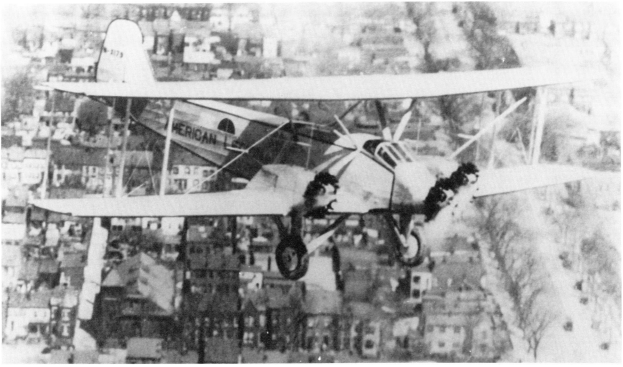

29

28. On September 21, 1926, the Sikorsky S-35 lumbered down the runway at Roosevelt Field with Fonck and three additional crew members, headed for Paris. Unfortunately, they never even made it out of Roosevelt Field. An auxiliary wheel broke loose from its housing, causing the plane to sway. Mechanic Jacob Isliamoff then released the entire auxiliary-wheel system, but one wheel bounced up and damaged the elevator. As the plane neared the end of the runway it still had not gained sufficient speed to lift off, and the damaged elevator now would not work. Fonck was still trying to get the plane airborne when it went off the end of the runway and nosed over in the ditch separating Curtiss and Roosevelt Fields. The plane quickly burst into flames, incinerating two crewmen.

The Orteig Prize had claimed the first of its many victims. This photo shows the remains of the S-35 after the disaster. *(Photo: Cradle of Aviation Museum.)*

29. Next to vie for the Orteig Prize were Naval officers Noel Davis and Stanton Wooster, who refitted an old Keystone bomber named the *American Legion* (seen here) with new Wright engines. On April 26, 1927, while taking off from Langley Field, Virginia, on a test flight with a heavy load of fuel, the overburdened plane was unable to remain in the air and plummeted into a swamp, killing Davis and Wooster. The elusive prize had claimed two more lives. *(Photo: Cradle of Aviation Museum.)*

30

30. Davis and Wooster's *American Legion* after crashing. *(Photo: Cradle of Aviation Museum.)*

31. In 1927 famous French war ace Charles Nungesser attempted to win the Orteig Prize and the fame it promised. Along with navigator François Coli, Nungesser took off from Le Bourget Field, Paris, on May 8, 1927, in a modified Levavasseur bomber named *L'Oiseau Blanc* ("The White Bird"), seen here. Nungesser and Coli had not obtained adequate information on the weather before leaving Paris. Five hours after takeoff, rain, snow, ice and 25-mph headwinds were reported for the western Atlantic Ocean. *L'Oiseau Blanc* had no radio and was never seen again. *(Photo: Cradle of Aviation Museum.)*

31

32

32. The construction of the Ryan "NYP" monoplane named by
    Lindbergh the *Spirit of St. Louis* began at the Ryan plant (a
    former fish cannery!) in San Diego on February 28, 1927. The
    NYP (for "New York to Paris") was based on Ryan's success-
    ful M-2 mail plane. Work proceeded day and night, seven days
    a week, for two months. Here, the steel-tubing fuselage
    framework is all welded up and ready for installation of the
    engine. *(Photo: National Air and Space Museum.)*

33. The large main fuel tank (there were also four auxiliary
    tanks) as installed in the frame of the *Spirit*. This tank, placed
    between the engine and the pilot, blocked all forward vision,
    but was aerodynamically efficient and safer for the pilot in the
    event of a crash. *(Photo: Ev Cassagneres Collection.)*

34. The *Spirit* at a later stage of construction. Now its Wright
    J-5 engine and oil tank have been installed. Note also the elas-
    tic bungee shock absorbers on the landing gear, which will be
    faired over. *(Photo: Ev Cassagneres Collection.)*

33

34

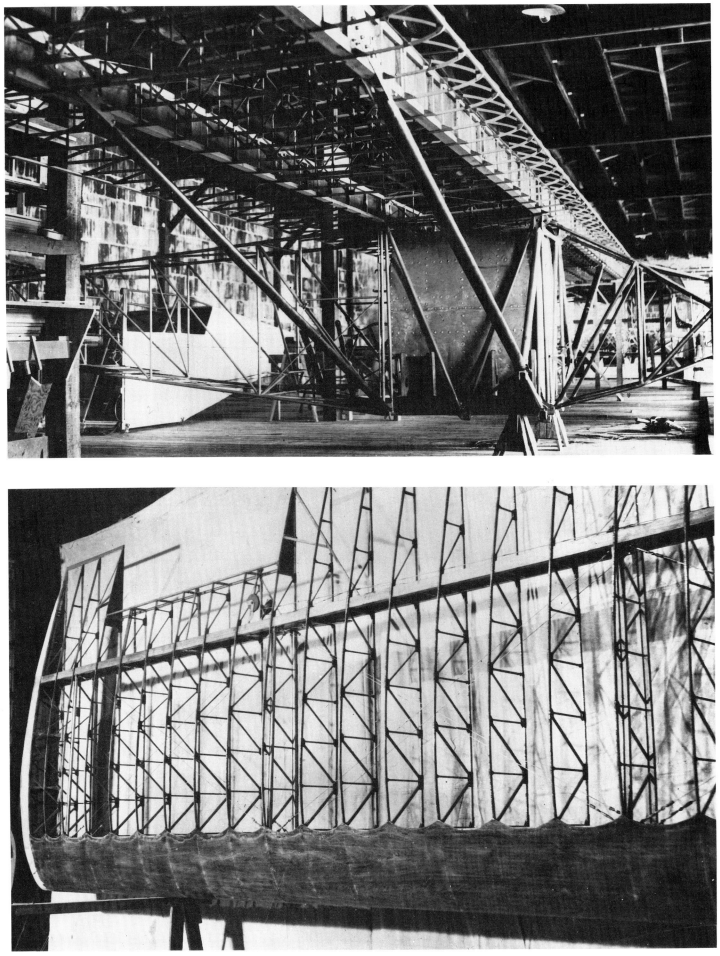

35. TOP: The wings being "mated" to the fuselage. The struts extending from the fuselage to the wings not only braced the wings, they also shifted to the lower fuselage and wings the heavy load placed on the landing gear during takeoff. BOTTOM: Closeup of the wooden truss-type wing-rib construction. The wood is mostly spruce; it will next be covered with cotton cloth, doped and painted. *(Photos: National Air and Space Museum.)*

36. View of the cockpit of the *Spirit*. The main fuel tank and instrument panel, blocking all forward vision, are the most prominent in this photo. The largest lever on the left is for trimming the tail. Throttle and carburetor-heater controls are to the left of that. A magnetic compass hangs above the wicker pilot's seat (not visible here). Note the complicated array of fourteen valves below the instrument panel to control the five fuel tanks. Lindbergh was confined to this space for over 33 hours. *(Photo: National Air and Space Museum.)*

37. A closeup view of the instrument panel of the *Spirit*. In the center near the top is the earth-inductor compass, which gave a more accurate reading than a magnetic compass. Altimeter, airspeed indicator and clock are on the right side. The rectangular opening to the left of center is the periscope; the lever at its left slid it in and out. At the left on the panel is the fuel-mixture control. At the bottom, center, is an instrument like a carpenter's level that showed the airplane's attitude (the artificial horizon had not yet been invented). *(Photo: Cradle of Aviation Museum.)*

36

37

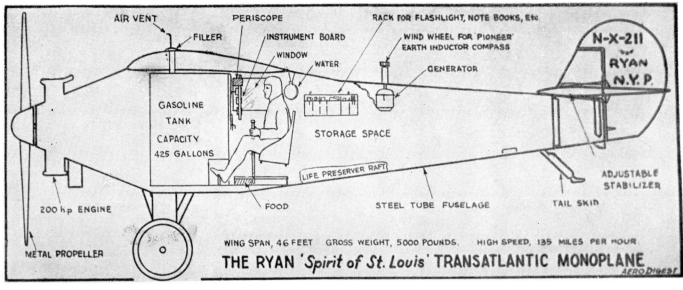

38

39

38. Cutaway view of the *Spirit of St. Louis*. The way that the main fuel tank blocks the pilot's vision is clearly seen here. This drawing reveals the purely functional, yet elegant, engineering of the *Spirit*.

39. The wing of the *Spirit* after being taken out of the second story of the Ryan plant. It was first slid onto a boxcar, then lowered to the ground. The man in the dark suit standing on top of the boxcar is Lindbergh, supervising the operation. *(Photo: Ev Cassagneres Collection.)*

40

40. The Ryan workers who built the *Spirit of St. Louis* pose in front of their handiwork. Lindbergh stands seventh from the left. Seventh from the right is welder Douglas Corrigan, the same man who would "accidentally" fly across the Atlantic Ocean to Ireland in 1938, earning himself the name "Wrong Way" Corrigan. *(Photo: National Air and Space Museum.)*

41. The *Spirit* ready for flight testing after being towed to Dutch Flats, a natural (and obviously unpaved!) airfield near San Diego. It will soon head east, for St. Louis, New York and Paris. *(Photo: National Air and Space Museum.)*

41

42

42. A modified "Keep Out" sign posted in front of the hangar at Dutch Flats. *(Photo: National Air and Space Museum.)*

43. The finished *Spirit of St. Louis* before flight testing at North Island, San Diego. Chief flight mechanic Harm Jon van der Linde fuels the plane (note funnel) as Lindbergh stands with Ryan workers O. R. McNeel, George Hammond, Donald Hall (Ryan's chief engineer and the main designer of the *Spirit*) and A. J. Edwards. Lindbergh's funds were tight, and the fuel

was supplied free in exchange for this publicity photo. *(Photo: National Air and Space Museum.)*

44. Lindbergh and the *Spirit* at Rockwell Field, North Island, San Diego, on May 10, after flying in from nearby Dutch Flats. Later on this day Lindbergh would depart on the long overnight flight to St. Louis. *(Photo: National Air and Space Museum.)*

43

44

45

46

47

45. The *Spirit of St. Louis*, at 3:55 P.M. on May 10, departing from Rockwell Field for St. Louis. The lack of a carburetor heater caused serious engine misfiring as the plane climbed to a chilly 12,000 feet to cross the mountains at night.

46. Lindbergh and the *Spirit* on May 11, 1927, at Lambert Field, St. Louis, after the 14 hour, 25 minute flight from San Diego. After the problem with the carburetor had almost caused a serious accident, Lindbergh made up his mind to have a carburetor heater installed in New York. *(Photo: Cradle of Aviation Museum.)*

47. Despite his problems on the flight between San Diego and St. Louis, Lindbergh set a new speed record between the two cities. Many friends and aviators, including the Robertson brothers, were on hand to greet him in St. Louis. Here the Wright J-5 engine is being inspected by Charles Lawrance, the engine's designer. *(Photo: Cradle of Aviation Museum.)*

48. The St. Louis businessmen who backed Lindbergh's flight also met him at Lambert Field. Here, E. Lansing Ray looks over the plane. Lindbergh was grateful that his business associates released him from dinner and speaking engagements so he could get an early start for New York the next morning. *(Photo: Cradle of Aviation Museum.)*

48

49

49. Lindbergh after arriving in New York. He landed at Curtiss Field at 5:33 P.M. on May 12. His flying time from San Diego had been 21 hours, 40 minutes, a new transcontinental speed record. Before landing he circled over the three adjacent airfields, Curtiss Field, Roosevelt Field and Mitchel Field, observing immediately that Roosevelt Field had the longest runway. Upon landing, Lindbergh was surprised when he was mobbed by a crowd of several hundred people, including many from the news media. It was his first exposure to journalists—an unpleasant one. *(Photo: Cradle of Aviation Museum.)*

50

51

50. Hangar 16 at Curtiss Field (immediately west of Roosevelt Field), in which the *Spirit of St. Louis* was stored the week before the flight. This photograph was taken long afterward. *(Photo: Cradle of Aviation Museum.)*

51. Inside Hangar 16 the week before the flight, with the *Spirit*

under the watchful eye of the guard at the left (it was never left unattended). Work done in this hangar included the installation of a new compass and carburetor heater, tuning up the engine, and checking all fuel and oil lines for leaks. The Wright company had mechanics waiting for Lindbergh on the field. *(Photo: Cradle of Aviation Museum.)*

53. While he was in New York, Lindbergh's ever-watchful mother came in from Detroit to see him. Here they pose with the *Spirit* for photographers. *(Photo: Cradle of Aviation Museum.)*

52. The classic shot of Lindbergh and the *Spirit* at Curtiss Field. Notice that the propeller's spinner, which had been removed in St. Louis or lost in flight, has not yet been replaced. *(Photo: Cradle of Aviation Museum.)*

54. Lindbergh working on the nine-cylinder, 220-hp Wright J-5 "Whirlwind" engine in Hangar 16. The propeller and spinner have temporarily been removed. *(Photo: Cradle of Aviation Museum.)*

53

52

55

56

55. The *Spirit* rests on the open expanse of Curtiss Field prior to a test flight, shortly before the flight to Paris. Lindbergh and his plane were routinely surrounded by onlookers every time it was rolled out of the hangar. *(Photo: Frank Strnad Collection.)*

56. Rival for the Orteig Prize: the Bellanca *Columbia*, at Roosevelt Field, May 1927. Owned by Charles Levine and flown by Clarence Chamberlin, the plane was grounded by legal problems when Lindbergh took off. However, on June 4, with Chamberlin at the controls and Levine in the passenger's seat (history's first trans-Atlantic airplane passenger), the *Columbia* took off on a partly successful nonstop flight across the ocean. Prior to Lindbergh's departure, "New York to Paris" had been painted on the fuselage. Then "Paris" was painted over and their new destination left a secret. Eventually "Berlin" replaced Paris. The *Columbia* made it to Germany but not to Berlin, at least not without stopping first. *(Photo: Cradle of Aviation Museum.)*

57. Clarence Chamberlin (left), one of the most respected fliers of the day, and Charles Levine in front of their Bellanca. A court injunction had held up their flight for weeks. It seems that the eccentric owner Levine had been wrangling with a number of prospective pilots before deciding on Chamberlin. In addition, at the last minute he bumped the navigator and decided to go on the flight himself as a passenger. Levine, last of the early trans-Atlantic fliers, died in relative obscurity in 1992. *(Photo: Cradle of Aviation Museum.)*

58. Another rival for trans-Atlantic honors: Comdr. Richard Byrd with his Fokker Trimotor *America* on the takeoff ramp at Roosevelt Field, May 1927. (Byrd did not actually enter for the Orteig Prize, however.) Judging that weather conditions were unacceptable the morning Lindbergh took off for Paris, Byrd elected not to go. Finally, on June 29, Byrd and a crew of three took off for Paris. After finding Paris in the dark (but not the airfield), they managed to land in the water off the coast of France. *(Photo: Cradle of Aviation Museum.)*

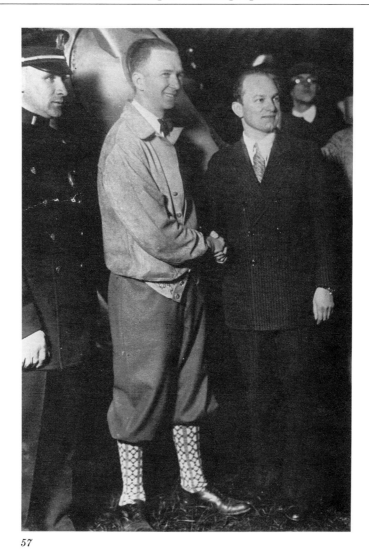

57

59

59. While working on the *Spirit*, and waiting for the weather to clear, Lindbergh often had visitors from rival camps in his hangar. The rivalry was friendly, as each knew what the others were up against. Here Commander Byrd and Clarence Chamberlin greet Lindbergh. Note that Byrd's left wrist is in a cast; he had broken it a few weeks before in a test-flight crash. *(Photo: Cradle of Aviation Museum.)*

60

61

62

60. At Curtiss Field, famous French World War I "flying ace" René Fonck calls on Lindbergh to wish him good luck.

61. At Curtiss Field Lindbergh befriended a stray cat he named Patsy. At first he thought of taking Patsy with him but later decided against it, claiming that such a dangerous flight was an unjustifiable risk of the cat's life. More likely, he had no desire to carry the extra weight.

62. In this staged press photo Lindbergh and Clarence Chamberlin discuss flight routes at the Garden City Hotel, where both stayed before their flights. *(Photo: Cradle of Aviation Museum.)*

63. The Garden City Hotel in 1927. All the trans-Atlantic competitors who started out on this side of the ocean stayed here
before their flights. Just minutes from Roosevelt Field, this
was the finest hotel on Long Island at the time. In the 1970's
the old building was demolished and replaced with a newer,
larger structure. *(Photo courtesy of the Nassau County
Museum.)*

64. During the week Lindbergh was at Curtiss Field, he made
several test flights in the *Spirit* to check out the new compass
and carburetor heater, as well as the takeoff route, among
other things. Here the *Spirit* is being pushed out for the test
flight of May 14. On this flight Lindbergh established opti-
mum fuel-mixture settings with the help of Wright engineers.
Note the old Jennys in the background. *(Photo: National Air
and Space Museum.)*

65. Running up the *Spirit* prior to a test flight. Lindbergh can
just barely be made out in the cockpit. *(Photo: Court
Commercial Photo/Cradle of Aviation Museum.)*

66. Taking off on a test flight from Curtiss Field. This is often
identified as a photograph of the actual takeoff, but it is not,
as the propeller has no streamlined spinner on it. The original
spinner, made by Ryan and signed by its builders, was
removed in St. Louis or fell off in flight after Lindbergh left
for New York. While hangared at Curtiss Field, a Curtiss
metalsmith fabricated a new nose cone free of charge. The
new spinner did not have the burnishing of the old one but it
is the one that made the flight, remained on the *Spirit* ever
since, and now may be seen at the National Air and Space
Museum. *(Photo: Court Commercial Photo/Cradle of
Aviation Museum.)*

63

64

65

66

67

68

67. On May 19, 1927, the weather was so bad that Lindbergh was convinced that he couldn't take off the next day, so he decided to go on a short tour of the area with friends. Shown here (from left to right) are public-relations man Harry Bruno, Frank Mahoney (co-owner of the Ryan Aircraft Corporation), an unknown chorus girl, Lindbergh and another P.R. man, Dick Blythe. They visited the Wright factory in New Jersey and planned on seeing a Broadway show that evening. However, a last-minute call to the meteorologist had them hustling back to Curtiss Field, as the weather over the Atlantic seemed to be clearing. They never saw the show. Note that Lindbergh is still wearing his flying pants, the only pair of pants he brought to New York. *(Photo: Cradle of Aviation Museum.)*

68, Unable to sleep, Lindbergh arrived at Curtiss Field at about
69. 3 A.M. These photos were taken at approximately 5 A.M. The *Spirit*'s tail wheel rests on a flatbed truck, and, with police

escort, the plane is being towed about a mile up the hill to neighboring Roosevelt Field. The plane was partially fueled before leaving the hangar. Final fueling would be done at the end of the runway. Lindbergh said the somber procession to Roosevelt Field reminded him of a funeral. Along the way they passed the Byrd and Chamberlin camps where, no doubt, they were relieved to see no sign of activity. *(Photos: National Air and Space Museum.)*

70. In this photo, the *Spirit* now sits at the end of the mile-long runway. It was drizzly and overcast and the runway was muddy. The engine was covered with a blanket to keep out the dampness. Slowly, from five-gallon cans, the last of 450 gallons of fuel were put in. The *Spirit* had never taken off with a full load of gasoline. In all, fully loaded, the plane weighed two and a half tons. *(Photo: National Air and Space Museum.)*

69

70

71

72

71. Charles Lawrance, designer of the J-5 engine that would carry Lindbergh across the ocean, comes to see him off. *(Photo: Cradle of Aviation Museum.)*

72. At about 7:40 A.M., Lindbergh dons his flying suit. *(Photo: Cradle of Aviation Museum.)*

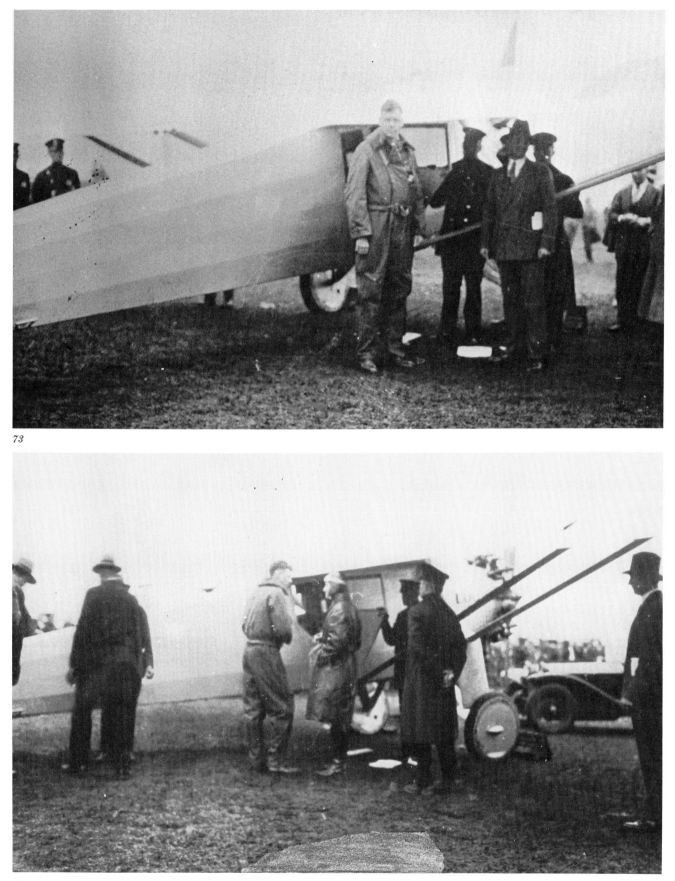

73

74

73. Now in his flying suit, Lindbergh is being bid farewell by well-wishers who have come to see him off. Policemen were guarding the runway while Wright mechanics checked the engine. Lindbergh knew that an engine failure immediately after takeoff would mean certain death in a blazing inferno. Harry Guggenheim, aviation philanthropist and, later, long-time friend of Lindbergh's, stands next to him in this photo.

Guggenheim told Lindbergh to "look me up" when he got back. *(Photo: Cradle of Aviation Museum.)*

74. Commander Byrd, who would attempt the flight to Paris a month later, now comes over to wish Lindbergh luck. *(Photo: Cradle of Aviation Museum.)*

75

76

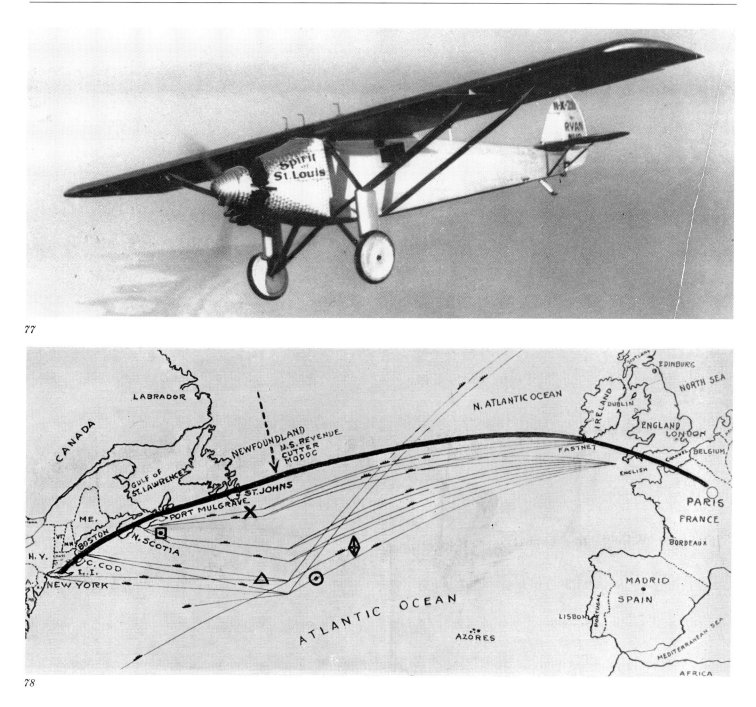

77

78

75. On May 20, 1927, at about 7:50 A.M., the *Spirit of St. Louis* sat at the end of Roosevelt Field's muddy runway, as seen in this photo. About 150 people crowded around the plane, waiting to see if Lindbergh would get off safely. Lindbergh climbed into the cockpit, buckled his belt, pulled down his goggles and peered out of the left window. *(Photo: Cradle of Aviation Museum.)*

76. After waving away the chocks, Lindbergh opened the engine full-throttle. The airplane hardly moved because of the overload and heavy mud. Mechanics and spectators rushed forward and pushed on the wing struts to get the plane moving. The *Spirit* gradually gained speed and barely lifted off the ground. It actually sank back to the runway twice before gaining sufficient flying speed. Lindbergh cleared the telephone wires and trees at the end of the runway by only twenty feet. After he had passed Newfoundland, there was no news of him for 16 hours. The world stood in awe as he flew on alone, fighting exhaustion and bad weather for much of the

way. When he finally saw Ireland, Lindbergh felt that he knew how the dead would feel to be alive again. The "Flyin' Fool" had now become the "Lone Eagle." *(Photo: Cradle of Aviation Museum.)*

77. This is not a picture of the *Spirit* en route to Paris. No such picture exists. The present photo was most likely taken during a test flight in San Diego, and it at least gives us an idea of what the *Spirit* would have looked like heading out over the North Atlantic. *(Photo: Cradle of Aviation Museum.)*

78. The dark line shows Lindbergh's course across the Atlantic. He was last seen over North America at St. John's, Newfoundland, at 7:15 P.M. (Eastern Daylight Time). The Great Circle route that Lindbergh pioneered accounted for the curvature of the earth and was thus a shorter path to Europe than a "straight" line would have been. Other lines on this map show the regular shipping lanes.

79. At 10:22 P.M. (local time), May 21, 1927, Lindbergh arrived at Le Bourget Field in Paris. When the plane stopped, he was shocked to see 100,000 screaming Parisians converging on him in a scene of mass hysteria. He had had no idea whether anyone at all would be there to greet him! *(Photo: Cradle of Aviation Museum.)*

80. To protect it from irresponsible souvenir hunters, Lindbergh's plane was towed inside this hangar and surrounded by French soldiers. *(Photo: National Air and Space Museum.)*

81. Before it could be secured, the *Spirit* had already been seriously damaged. Souvenir hunters had torn off pieces of fabric, damaged wooden stringers and stolen an engine fitting.

81

80

82. Here the fuselage has been stripped of the torn fabric that had remained. It had to be completely re-covered before the plane could be flown again. *(Photo: Cradle of Aviation Museum.)*

83. On May 22, after his first sleep in two and a half days, Charles Lindbergh waves to a huge crowd from a balcony outside the American Embassy in Paris. *(Photo: National Air and Space Museum.)*

84. At the entrance to the Embassy, Ambassador Myron T. Herrick (right) leads a cheer for Lindbergh. They were both surprised at the intensity of the pro-American fervor. *(Photo: Cradle of Aviation Museum.)*

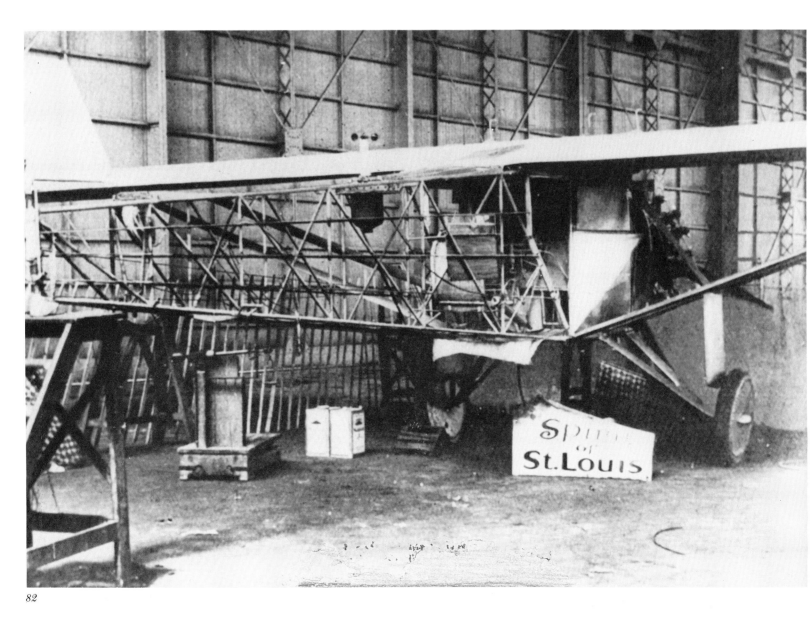

82

83

84

86

85

87

85. On May 23, Lindbergh visited the Elysée Palace, where he
was awarded the medal of the Legion of Honor, seen here
pinned to his lapel. Ambassador Herrick stands to the right of
Lindbergh. *(Photo: National Air and Space Museum.)*

86. Analogous to the first satellite photographs of recent years,
this fuzzy photograph, taken on May 23, was the first to be
transmitted by radio from Europe to America. From left to
right: Lindbergh, Ambassador Herrick and French President
Gaston Doumergue.

87. Lindbergh with Louis Blériot, the French aviator who in 1909
had been the first to fly across the English Channel. *(Photo:
Cradle of Aviation Museum.)*

88. In France Lindbergh also met Marshal Foch (right), who had
been commander of the Allied Armies in World War I.

88

89

90

89. On May 27, when he returned to Le Bourget Field, Lindbergh was greeted by the 34th Regiment of the French Flying Division. *(Photo: National Air and Space Museum.)*

90. At Le Bourget, Lindbergh had a chance to try out the latest French fighter, seen here behind him, a Nieuport 29C with a 300-hp engine. *(Photo: National Air and Space Museum.)*

91. The *Spirit of St. Louis* near the Seine River in Paris. The bridge is the Pont Alexandre III. The prominent buildings at the right are the Grand Palais and the Petit Palais. *(Photo: National Air and Space Museum.)*

91

92

93

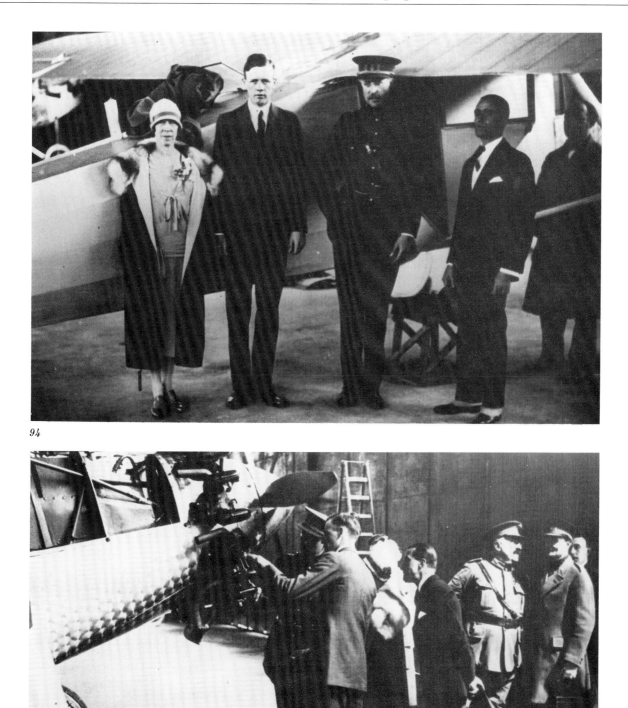

94

95

92. The *Spirit of St. Louis* over French farmland. Lindbergh was on his way to Brussels, Belgium. *(Photo: National Air and Space Museum.)*

93. At Evere Aerodrome near Brussels. The crowd was a bit less unruly there than the one at Paris had been. *(Photo: National Air and Space Museum.)*

94. Lindbergh posing with Queen Elizabeth and King Albert of Belgium. The royal couple were both fliers and enthusiastic patrons of aviation, and it was the King himself who showed Lindbergh the latest types of Belgian planes. *(Photo: National Air and Space Museum.)*

95. Here Lindbergh in his turn shows the *Spirit of St. Louis* to King Albert and Queen Elizabeth. *(Photo: National Air and Space Museum.)*

96. On May 29, Lindbergh flew to England. At Croydon Aerodrome, London, he was faced with a crowd of 150,000, larger than the one that had greeted him in Paris, which made landing very difficult. This photograph is a composite, retouched at the time; nevertheless, it accurately reveals the extent of the crowd. *(Photo: Cradle of Aviation Museum.)*

97. After 1,200 police managed to restrain the crowd, the *Spirit of St. Louis* was at last able to land at Croydon. *(Photo: National Air and Space Museum.)*

98. Once the *Spirit* was on the ground, it was engulfed. It was with difficulty that the police protected Lindbergh from the crowd. *(Photo: National Air and Space Museum.)*

96

97

98

99. Lindbergh in the middle of the mob (within circled area). Finally officials of the Royal Air Club whisked him away in their car.

100. From a balcony at Croydon, Lindbergh gave a brief speech. His unassuming, genial nature captured British hearts.

101. Lindbergh passes through Trafalgar Square in the heart of London. *(Photo: National Air and Space Museum.)*

102. Lindbergh at the Albert Hall in London on May 31. Second from the right in the foreground stands the Prince of Wales, the future King Edward VIII. *(Photo: Cradle of Aviation Museum.)*

100

99

101

102

103

104

103. Lindbergh had wanted to tour Europe a while longer, but President Coolidge thought that it was time for him to return to the United States—safely, by a navy cruiser, the U.S.S. *Memphis*, with the *Spirit* stowed below. Here, on board the *Memphis*, a sailor presents him with a homemade model of the *Spirit*. *(Photo: Cradle of Aviation Museum.)*

104. Lindbergh disembarking in Norfolk, Virginia (the seaport closest to Washington), on June 11. His mother, who had traveled to Washington to greet him and had boarded the ship earlier, follows him down the gangplank in this photograph. *(Photo: Cradle of Aviation Museum.)*

105. The *Spirit of St. Louis* being brought on shore after having been removed from the *Memphis* on June 11. *(Photo: Ev Cassagneres Collection.)*

106. Lindbergh in the rear of his car in the triumphal parade down Pennsylvania Avenue in Washington. *(Photo: Cradle of Aviation Museum.)*

107. In a ceremony at the foot of the Washington Monument, attended by 250,000 people, President Calvin Coolidge awarded Lindbergh the Distinguished Flying Cross. Here he is seen pinning the medal on Lindbergh's lapel. Searching for a way to honor Lindbergh for his accomplishment, Congress specially voted this award into existence for the occasion. *(Photo: Cradle of Aviation Museum.)*

107

106

109

108

108. Here, on Sunday, June 12, Lindbergh lays a wreath on the Tomb of the Unknown Soldier at Arlington National Cemetery. *(Photo: Cradle of Aviation Museum.)*

109. Later on June 12, distinguished jurist Charles Evans Hughes presented Lindbergh with the Cross of Honor, as seen here before the Capitol. *(Photo: Cradle of Aviation Museum.)*

110

110. Lindbergh with his mother, returning from the ceremony at the Capitol. Inset in this old news photograph is a "Welcome Home" poster created for the occasion. *(Photo: Cradle of Aviation Museum.)*

111. On June 13, when Lindbergh flew from Washington to Mitchel Field, Long Island, and then to New York harbor, he paused to have his picture taken with the distinguished aero-

nautical engineer Grover Loening (at right) standing in front of the *San Francisco*, the amphibious plane that Loening designed. *(Photo: National Air and Space Museum.)*

112. Lindbergh on board the *San Francisco*. This plane, the private aircraft of Gen. Mason Patrick, head of the Army Air Corps, had previously been flown around South America. *(Photo: National Air and Space Museum.)*

111

112

113

115

113. Seagoing vessels of all kinds greet Lindbergh on his arrival in New York. *(Photo: Cradle of Aviation Museum.)*

114. From a Staten Island ferry, reporters and spectators wave to Lindbergh as he flies overhead in the *San Francisco. (Photo: Cradle of Aviation Museum.)*

115. Lindbergh sits in the pilot's seat of the Loening amphibian. At the right is Capt. Ira Eaker. Now in New York harbor, Lindbergh is about to transfer to New York City's official yacht, the *Macom. (Photo: National Air and Space Museum.)*

114

116

116, On board the *Macom.* Lindbergh is about to receive a hero's
117. welcome in New York. *(Photo: Cradle of Aviation Museum.)*

118. The crowd cheers as Lindbergh passes up Lafayette Street, New York. *(Photo: Hank Anholzer Collection.)*

119. The full effect of the ticker-tape parade in lower Manhattan. It was estimated that 4.3 million people greeted Lindbergh and 1,800 tons of ticker tape were dropped onto the streets— a "blizzard" of paper, according to some viewers! *(Photo: Cradle of Aviation Museum.)*

120. Some of the floats on Broadway at Twenty-seventh Street, including a model of the *Spirit* and one of the Eiffel Tower. *(Photo: Cradle of Aviation Museum.)*

118

120

121

123

121. People crowded on top of this streetcar just to catch a glimpse of Lindbergh as he passed by.

122. At City Hall, Mayor James J. Walker, pinning a medal on Lindbergh, said, "I don't give it to you—you won it!" *(Photo: Cradle of Aviation Museum.)*

123. The parade as it moved past the Library on Fifth Avenue at Forty-second Street. *(Photo: Cradle of Aviation Museum.)*

122

124. When the procession reached Central Park at 5 P.M., after five hours, another 300,000 people greeted Lindbergh. In a ceremony in the Park, Governor Alfred Smith (at left in this photo) awarded Lindbergh the Medal of Honor of the State of New York. Through a special NBC hookup, Lindbergh's voice was heard over 54 radio stations in 24 states. The number of listeners was estimated at thirty million—the most that had listened to a single broadcast up to that time. *(Photo: Glen Apfelbaum Collection.)*

125. After eight years and many lost lives, the Orteig Prize was finally awarded. In this photo, Raymond Orteig himself (with the mustache, to the right of Lindbergh) looks on as Col. Walter Scott, on behalf of the Orteig Prize Trustees, pins a medal on Lindbergh. *(Photo: Cradle of Aviation Museum.)*

124

125

126

127

126. The check awarded by Raymond Orteig.

127. Early on June 16, Lindbergh flew to Washington in an Army plane to pick up the *Spirit of St. Louis*. Here, on his return to New York later that day, he greets officers of the Nassau County Police Department Motorcycle Division at Mitchel Field. A huge reception awaited him at neighboring Roosevelt Field, where his adventure had begun less than three weeks before. *(Photo: Cradle of Aviation Museum.)*

128

128. This aerial photograph, taken at 3:30 P.M. on June 16, shows
the turnout that awaited the returning hero. Arranged in con-
centric circles are hundreds of parked automobiles. The dirt
runway that Lindbergh took off from stretches from the left
in this photo, through the circles of cars, diagonally up and to
the right. *(Photo: National Air and Space Museum.)*

129

129. The speaker's platform in a sea of people at Roosevelt Field. In one of the hangars far to the rear in the photo is the *America*, which, flown by Comdr. Richard Byrd and crew, would take off for France in thirteen days. *(Photo: Glen Apfelbaum Collection.)*

130

131

132

133

130. Lindbergh addressing the crowd at Roosevelt Field. *(Photo: Cradle of Aviation Museum.)*

131. The following day, June 17, Lindbergh flew the *Spirit of St. Louis* back to the city for which it was named. Eight businessmen from St. Louis had provided the financial backing for Lindbergh's flight in the first place. Here, at Lambert Field, Lindbergh is greeted by Mayor Victor Miller and members of the Missouri National Guard. *(Photo: Missouri Historical Society.)*

132. A tired-looking Charles Lindbergh late in the day on June 17. Earlier, after a huge parade, the Secretary of War had awarded him a promotion to colonel in the Army Air Corps Reserve. *(Photo: Cradle of Aviation Museum.)*

133. As he left St. Louis on June 19, Lindbergh treated his well-wishers with an exhibition flight over the World's Fair grounds, as seen here.

134

135

134. After his flight to Paris, Lindbergh was presented with many gifts. Of those with substantial intrinsic value, the only one he accepted was this 1927 Franklin touring car. At the time he didn't own an automobile; in return, he posed for this photograph, which was good publicity for the manufacturer. *(Photo: Cradle of Aviation Museum.)*

135. "Falaise," the Guggenheim mansion on Sands Point, Long Island, New York. Here, Lindbergh was a frequent guest of Harry and Carol Guggenheim, who were staunch supporters of aviation. After the initial round of post-flight celebrations, Lindbergh spent time in this Norman-style mansion writing an account of his adventure that was hastily brought out as the book *We* (1927). *(Photo: Nassau County Museum.)*

136. Lindbergh and the *Spirit* at Mitchel Field, Long Island, on July 20, 1927, at the beginning of a new adventure. Just a month after the end of the original celebrations in New York, Washington and St. Louis, Lindbergh, encouraged and aided by his friend Harry Guggenheim, embarked on an ambitious nationwide tour in the *Spirit of St. Louis*. Eighty-two stops were planned, and all forty-eight states covered. Landings were made at the scheduled time of 2 P.M. at every stop (with one understandable exception, fogbound Portland, Maine). Lindbergh also dropped greetings over 192 other places. For a full three months, the excitement of the New York-Paris-flight celebrations was extended. More important, the reliability and safety of air transportation were dramatically demonstrated. *(Photo: Cradle of Aviation Museum.)*

137. This map shows the route of Lindbergh's national tour, as well as that of a "Pan-American" tour he took at the end of the year. The first stop was at Hartford, Connecticut.

136

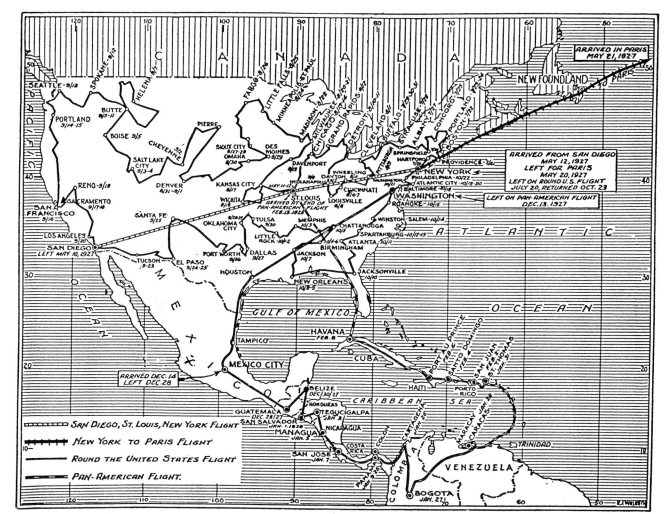

137

139

138

138. Lindbergh in the *Spirit* at Mitchel Field. *(Photo: Cradle of Aviation Museum.)*

139. Orchard Beach, Maine. After circling the vicinity of fogbound Portland for an hour and a half, Lindbergh was forced to land here instead. The next day he successfully reached Portland. *(Photo: National Air and Space Museum.)*

140. At the mountaintop airfield in Springfield, Vermont, July 26, 1927. *(Photo: Ev Cassagneres Collection.)*

141. Lindbergh with Mayor John Boyd Thacher of Albany, New York, on July 27. In a typical visit, Lindbergh was greeted with pomp and ceremony. He briefly addressed a huge crowd, as always confining the subject of his talk to the promotion of aviation, and soon was off again. *(Photo: Cradle of Aviation Museum.)*

140

141

142A

142. On August 6, Lindbergh touched down at Cincinnati, Ohio. Before he left, he let Phil Love, his old buddy from Army flying-school days, pilot the *Spirit* for ten minutes over the airfield shown here. *(Photo: National Air and Space Museum.)*

142A. On August 11, in Detroit, Lindbergh took Henry Ford for his first airplane ride. Soon afterward, Lindbergh would be test-piloting planes built by Ford for Transcontinental Air Transport (TAT).

142

143. On August 12, in Grand Rapids, Michigan, Lindbergh took his mother for her first and only ride in the *Spirit*. Whenever he took anyone for a flight his passenger had to sit on the arm of his seat, as did his mother on this occasion, since the *Spirit* had only one seat. *(Photo: National Air and Space Museum.)*

144. Here Lindbergh addresses the gathered throng in Chicago on August 13. Although the crowd was intoxicated with joy at the mere sight of him, his message about the future of aviation ultimately got through: new airports were built, and airlines and the airmail flourished. *(Photo: Cradle of Aviation Museum.)*

144

143

145

146

145. August 18, somewhere in Kansas or Missouri. Over desolate stretches of land he would often drop down to within a few feet of the ground to observe some feature of interest. The "Lone Eagle" never got over the thrill of flight and always preferred this kind of experience to being worshiped as a hero on the ground. *(Photo: National Air and Space Museum.)*

146. On the Great Plains, late August or early September. Lindbergh touched down at Fargo, North Dakota, on August 26, and Pierre, South Dakota, a few days later. *(Photo: National Air and Space Museum.)*

147. Late August, somewhere over Iowa, flying over the typically checkerboard-patterned farms of the Midwest. A number of aerial photos like this were taken from a Department of Commerce plane that accompanied Lindbergh on his tour. *(Photo: National Air and Space Museum.)*

148. Cheyenne, Wyoming, September 2. These local residents are obviously glad to be posing with the *Spirit of St. Louis. (Photo: National Air and Space Museum.)*

147

148

149. September 3: over the Rocky Mountains. Flying from Cheyenne to Salt Lake City took seven hours, thirty-five minutes. At one point Lindbergh took the *Spirit* up to twenty thousand feet—without oxygen! *(Photo: National Air and Space Museum.)*

150. Skimming over the waters of Yellowstone Lake, Yellowstone National Park, Wyoming, on September 7. *(Photo: National Air and Space Museum.)*

151. Over the mountains of the Pacific Northwest in mid-September. *(Photo: National Air and Space Museum.)*

149

150

151

152. The usual crowds assemble to view Lindbergh at the San Francisco Civic Center, September 16. *(Photo: Library of Congress.)*

153. Lindbergh arrived in Los Angeles on September 20. Here he poses with Hollywood stars Douglas Fairbanks, Mary Pickford ("America's Sweetheart") and Marion Davies.

154. On September 21, the *Spirit of St. Louis* returned to its birthplace—San Diego, California. The turnout for Lindbergh's arrival was typical, as seen in this photo.

155. The *Spirit* returned to Mitchel Field on October 23, 1927. On the way, Lindbergh saw this country as few others have seen it, from "New England's valleys dotted by white villages," as he later wrote, to "the crystal waters of Michigan's great lakes, Arizona's pastel deserts, Georgia's red cotton fields, the cascades and deep forests of the Oregon northwest." Memories of this tour no doubt inspired his later work in conservation, at least in part. All in all, Lindbergh covered 22,350 miles on this tour, in the flying time of 260 hours. He made 147 speeches and was seen by over thirty million Americans. *(Photo: Cradle of Aviation Museum.)*

154

155

156. At Teterboro Airport, New Jersey, in November 1927. Standing immediately to Lindbergh's left is Guy Vaughan (center of photograph), an executive at Wright Aeronautics and producer of the J-5 engine. At the far right is Harry Bruno, one of Lindbergh's public relations men at the time of the Paris flight. *(Photo: Cradle of Aviation Museum.)*

157. On November 14, 1927, 6,000 people gathered at Washington Auditorium to see President Coolidge award Lindbergh the Hubbard Gold Medal of the National Geographic Society. The medal, awarded for the eighth time in forty years, was for great explorers. Officials of the government and diplomatic corps, as well as famous fliers, were in attendance, the most distinguished audience ever to gather for such an occasion. *(Photo: Cradle of Aviation Museum.)*

157

156

158

159

158. Lindbergh had not been back from his national tour a full two months before he took off on another tour in the *Spirit of St. Louis*. At the invitation of the American Ambassador to Mexico, Dwight Morrow, he left Washington, D.C., on December 13, 1927. Twenty-seven and a half hours later the citizens of Mexico City watched him land at Val Buena Airport, as seen in this photograph. Bad weather conditions made this flight in some respects more dangerous than the one to Paris, but Lindbergh characteristically welcomed the challenge as an opportunity to test some new flying instruments. *(Photo: Cradle of Aviation Museum.)*

159. Lindbergh stayed two weeks in Mexico, where he met Anne Morrow, one of the Ambassador's daughters. In a year and a half Charles and Anne were married. In this photo, Mexican workers declare their appreciation of Mexican President Calles, Ambassador Morrow and Lindbergh. Lindbergh's reception in Mexico was as great as any had been in Europe or the United States, and the people turned out in enormous numbers. This was a triumph for Morrow, as Mexican-American relations had been very strained at the time.

160. After Mexico, Lindbergh continued to Guatemala and then on to thirteen other countries in a broad "Pan-American" tour that lasted approximately two months. Here the *Spirit* has just landed at "Campo Lindbergh," Panama. *(Photo: National Air and Space Museum.)*

161. Here he arrives at France Field, in the Canal Zone, Panama. *(Photo: National Air and Space Museum.)*

162. Lindbergh flies over the Gaillard Cut, part of the Panama Canal. *(Photo: National Air and Space Museum.)*

160

161

162

163. A panoramic view of the *Spirit of St. Louis* over Gatun Lake in the Canal Zone. *(Photo: National Air and Space Museum.)*

164. In Colón, Panama, Lindbergh received the usual tumultuous greeting. During his stay in Panama at one point it seemed that Lindbergh had disappeared. Actually, an American Army colonel had taken him on a hunting trip in the Panamanian jungle. He was glad to escape from the crowds for a few days. *(Photo: National Air and Space Museum.)*

165. Here, on January 25, 1928, at France Field, Lindbergh is flanked by the French aviators Lt. Dieudonné Costes (standing at the left of Lindbergh) and Lt. Joseph-Marie Le Brix (right). Distinguished in their own right, these fliers had recently flown nonstop from Africa to South America (a record), part of a 35,000-mile trip around the world that was to end at Mitchel Field, Long Island, on February 11, 1928. Posing with the three celebrities are officers of the U.S. Army Air Service, Lt. Col. Fisher (extreme left), Capt. Simonin (second from right) and Lt. Douglass (extreme right). *(Photo: National Air and Space Museum.)*

164

165

166

167

166. After leaving Panama, Lindbergh looped through Colombia and Venezuela and then up to St. Thomas in the Virgin Islands, where he is seen arriving in this photo. *(Photo: National Air and Space Museum.)*

167. Being greeted by Governor Waldo Evans on arrival on St. Thomas, January 31. In the next week Lindbergh flew to Puerto Rico, the Dominican Republic, Haiti and Cuba before returning to the U.S. On this last leg of the flight, he flew non-stop from Havana to St. Louis, where his Pan-American tour officially ended on February 13. *(Photo: National Air and Space Museum.)*

168. In Havana, Lindbergh was introduced to Juan Trippe, founder of Pan American Airways, with whom he was to have a long and fruitful relationship as a consultant. Here he sits in the cockpit of a Pan American airmail plane, a new Fokker F-VII Trimotor. *(Photo: Cradle of Aviation Museum.)*

168

169

170

169. As Lindbergh was, quite simply, the most famous pilot in the world, he was often asked to fly a wide variety of aircraft. Although he flew many types of planes, many at his own request, he refused to endorse any for commercial gain. Here he stands next to the prototype Curtiss "Robin" in 1928. On March 27, he flew this plane to St. Louis, where Curtiss had built a new production facility. *(Photo: Cradle of Aviation Museum.)*

170. Lindbergh with the "clipped-wing" Curtiss "Oriole" racing aircraft at Curtiss Field in 1928. This is apparently the plane used by field manager Casey Jones. The man at the right is C. M. Keyes, President of the Curtiss Aeroplane and Motor Corporation. *(Photo: Cradle of Aviation Museum.)*

171. The active life of the *Spirit of St. Louis* came to an end on April 30, 1928, when, keeping a promise, Lindbergh flew it from St. Louis to Bolling Field, Washington, D.C. This photograph shows the *Spirit*, wings having been separated from fuselage for shipping, arriving at the Smithsonian Institution, its last resting place. *(Photo: National Air and Space Museum.)*

171

172

172. The *Spirit* hanging in the Smithsonian's Arts and Industries Building, where it remained until it was moved to the new National Air and Space Museum in 1976. However reluctantly he parted with the *Spirit of St. Louis*, Lindbergh recognized that it was now a national treasure and belonged to the people of the United States. In subsequent years he would visit the Smithsonian incognito and just stand in a corner and stare at the plane that he had flown over 40,000 miles. *(Photo: National Air and Space Museum.)*

173

174

175

173. A closeup of the engine cowling, which had been specially decorated with flags of every nation that the *Spirit* had flown to.

174. The *Spirit of St. Louis* as it appears today, hanging in the "Milestones of Flight" gallery at the National Air and Space Museum. *(Photo: Dave Horn.)*

175. Ever the adventurer, and always willing to aid a friend in need, Lindbergh flew to Quebec in dangerous weather to deliver serum in an attempt to preserve the life of aviator Floyd Bennett. Bennett, already in poor health, had himself flown to Canada to aid three stranded European fliers; ironically, the Europeans survived but, despite Lindbergh's suc-

cessful arrival with the serum in April, Bennett, who had contracted pneumonia, lingered on for a few months and died on October 25, 1928. This photo shows Lindbergh about to depart for Quebec.

176. Lindbergh with Harry Guggenheim, in front of the latter's Loening amphibian, 1928. From the time of his return from Paris in 1927 through the 1930's, Lindbergh was good friends with Guggenheim, President of the Guggenheim Fund for the Promotion of Aeronautics, a philanthropic fund that in the 1930's probably furthered the cause of aviation more than any other factor. *(Photo: National Air and Space Museum.)*

176

177

178

177. Guggenheim's Loening amphibian in the water (1928). *(Photo: National Air and Space Museum.)*

178. Lindbergh adjusting the propeller of Guggenheim's plane (1928). *(Photo: National Air and Space Museum.)*

179. Lindbergh and Harry Guggenheim (left), this time standing before a Fokker F-10 Trimotor in a photo taken in May 1928. Guggenheim was involved in airline planning, and called upon Lindbergh as a consultant. The F-10 was Lindbergh's choice for the fledgling Western Air Express. *(Photo: Cradle of Aviation Museum.)*

180. Always in excellent physical shape, Lindbergh frequently engaged in strenuous exercise to stay that way. Here, in this photo taken in 1928 with Maj. Thomas G. Lamphier, commander of Selfridge Field, a military air base in Michigan, Lindbergh is headed for a swim in the lake.

179

180

181. Lindbergh with Capt. Emilio Carranza, the well-known
Mexican aviator, at Roosevelt Field, Long Island, in 1928.
Carranza, whom Lindbergh had met in Mexico a few months
earlier, was inspired by the flights of the *Spirit of St. Louis*
and purchased his own airplane from the Ryan Aircraft
Corporation. On June 12, shortly before this photograph was
taken, Carranza flew nonstop from Mexico City to
Washington, D.C., and then went on to New York. Carranza's
promising career was tragically cut short on the return flight,
however, when he crashed in a New Jersey thunderstorm and
was killed. *(Photo: Cradle of Aviation Museum.)*

182. An appealing shot of Lindbergh taken around this time.
(Photo: Cradle of Aviation Museum.)

183. Lindbergh with Ryan test pilot Red Harrigan in front of the
X-1 Ryan-Mahoney Special in 1928. Built in anticipation of a
civil-aeronautics boom after Lindbergh's Paris flight, the X-1
had several unique features, such as a moving stabilizer and
fin. Lindbergh test-flew the plane several times in St. Louis
and reportedly found it very touchy. The project soon showed
more problems than promise, and Mahoney dropped it at the
end of 1928. *(Photo: National Air and Space Museum.)*

184. In 1928 Franklin Mahoney of the Mahoney Aircraft Corporation (Mahoney, Ryan's former partner, had recently bought
him out) gave Lindbergh this Ryan "Brougham," registered
as number NX4215. The "X" meant that the plane was on the
leading edge of technology, with its larger wings and superior
landing lights. This plane had seats for four passengers, space
of which Lindbergh made frequent use. He also used the
plane on his early survey flights for Transcontinental Air
Transport. *(Photo: Cradle of Aviation Museum.)*

182

181

184

183

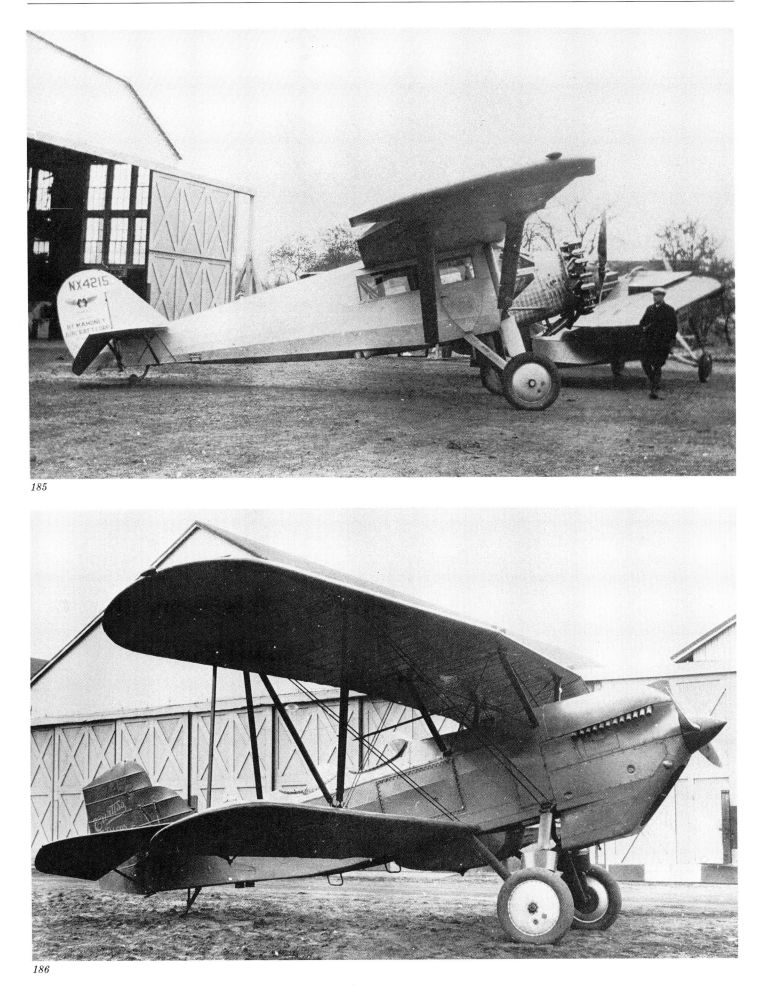

185

186

187

185. Lindbergh's Ryan Brougham at Curtiss Field, New York, in 1928. Despite its similarity to the *Spirit of St. Louis* (except for the far greater visibility all around), this plane was never favored by Lindbergh. After six months, he returned it to Mahoney when the Curtiss Corporation presented him with a Curtiss "Falcon." *(Photo: Cradle of Aviation Museum.)*

186. The special "Falcon" given to Lindbergh by Curtiss. Like the Brougham, it came in handy for the survey work Lindbergh was doing for TAT, although it had room for only one passenger. *(Photo: Cradle of Aviation Museum.)*

187. Lindbergh after arrival in Miami in the Falcon. *(Photo: Cradle of Aviation Museum.)*

188. Sixteen-year-old George Dade, high-school student, part-time employee at Curtiss Field, and aviation enthusiast, is seen in this 1928 photograph helping Lindbergh adjust his parachute. Forty-five years later, in 1973, the same George Dade, who had since become Founding Director of the Long Island Early Fliers Club, supervised the restoration of the original Curtiss Jenny that Lindbergh had barnstormed in in 1923. *(Photo: Cradle of Aviation Museum.)*

188

189

191. The *Columbus*, one of the first transcontinental airliners. One of the major operations for which Lindbergh was a consultant, Transcontinental Air Transport offered the first coast-to-coast service. Since night flying was still very dangerous, passengers had to continue their travel by train at night. Still, this was a beginning. *(Photo: National Air and Space Museum.)*

192. On Lindbergh's advice, TAT ordered a fleet of Ford Tri-Motors, the famed "Tin Goose." Here, Lindbergh is about to inaugurate the first coast-to-coast service in July 1929. *(Photo: National Air and Space Museum.)*

189. Wearing a white hat and standing to the left of Lindbergh in this photograph is one of the two men who started it all: Orville Wright. The occasion was the International Civil Aeronautics Conference in Washington, D.C. The date was December 13, 1928, four days before the twenty-fifth anniversary of the Wright brothers' first flight. *(Photo: Cradle of Aviation Museum.)*

190. Lindbergh with Anne Morrow, the woman he was about to marry, around the beginning of 1929. *(Photo: Cradle of Aviation Museum.)*

190

191

192

193. Lindbergh in the cockpit of the *City of Los Angeles*, the first plane to be part of the new transcontinental service. As Lindbergh's supervision of TAT's new national air network was widely known, a publicity agent conceived the idea of calling the airline "The Lindbergh Line." The name stuck. TAT later became TWA. *(Photo: National Air and Space Museum.)*

194. Lindbergh (second from left) at TAT's maintenance facility in Kansas City in 1929, inspecting a Wright J-5 engine that is in the process of being overhauled for use in the Ford Tri-Motor airliners. *(Photo: National Air and Space Museum.)*

195. As technical adviser to Pan American, Lindbergh enthusiastically supported the use of long-range flying boats. Here he is seen arriving in Belize City, British Honduras, in a Sikorsky S-38 on February 15, 1929. *(Photo: Cradle of Aviation Museum.)*

193

195

194

196. Closeup view of Lindbergh and the Sikorsky flying boat. *(Photo: Cradle of Aviation Museum.)*

197. Lindbergh and Anne Morrow in the Sikorsky flying boat. It was on this flight that they announced their engagement. Lindbergh later said that he liked Anne because she was the first woman who didn't try to talk to him the first time they met. *(Photo: Cradle of Aviation Museum.)*

198. A photo of Charles and Anne Lindbergh just before their marriage. *(Photo: Cradle of Aviation Museum.)*

196

197

198

199

199. Another photo of the Lindberghs, this one taken in September 1929. *(Photo: Cradle of Aviation Museum.)*

200. As a colonel in the Army Air Corps Reserve, Lindbergh was frequently associated with military aviation activities. Here he is seen with Brig. Gen. Benjamin Foulois at Mitchel Field (of which Foulois was then commanding officer), Long Island, New York, in 1929. Foulois had been taught to fly by Orville Wright in 1910, had seen distinguished service in World War I, and from 1931 to 1935 would serve as Chief of the Army Air Corps. *(Photo: Cradle of Aviation Museum.)*

201. On September 24, 1929, Lindbergh was present at one of the great events of aviation history: the "blind" flight of Lt. James H. ("Jimmy") Doolittle at Mitchel Field. *(Photo: Cradle of Aviation Museum.)*

200

201

202.

202. Lt. Doolittle's Consolidated NY-2 "Husky" biplane at the time of the flight. His field of vision obstructed by a hood, Doolittle flew a fifteen-mile course aided only by flying instruments. Air navigation would never be the same. *(Photo: Cradle of Aviation Museum.)*

203

204

203, 204. Lindbergh on board the aircraft carrier U.S.S. *Lexington* in 1929. The *Lexington*, commissioned in 1927 as the first of the second generation of American aircraft carriers, was capable of carrying 120 aircraft. After many years of service, it was sunk by the Japanese in 1942. *(Photos: John Colleary/Cradle of Aviation Museum.)*

205

206

207

205. This 1929 photo shows the trustees of the Guggenheim Fund; these men of vision helped change the course of American aviation. Standing, second from right, is Harry Guggenheim, with Lindbergh standing next to him. Standing on the other side of Lindbergh is Harry's father, Daniel Guggenheim, founder of the Fund. Seated, second from right, is Orville Wright. *(Photo: Cradle of Aviation Museum.)*

206. After a flight on a Keystone "Patrician" airliner in 1929. *(Photo: Cradle of Aviation Museum.)*

207. In 1929, on several occasions, Lindbergh led a Navy acrobatic team called the "High Hats," which performed at the Cleveland Air Races and elsewhere. Here he can be seen in a Boeing F2B-1 fighter, just prior to takeoff. Lindbergh was considered among the best acrobatic pilots in America at the time. *(Photo: Cradle of Aviation Museum.)*

208. Lindbergh in another Army Air Corps plane, 1929. *(Photo: Cradle of Aviation Museum.)*

209. In March 1930, the Lindberghs visited California to see about the delivery of a new plane. There, Hawley Bowlus, former Ryan factory manager from the *Spirit of St. Louis* days, invited them for a week of gliding off the Monterey Cliffs. Anne Lindbergh, here seen entering the cockpit of the glider, became the first woman to earn a glider pilot's license. *(Photo: Cradle of Aviation Museum.)*

210. Lindbergh in 1930, flying an Air Corps plane. He was a colonel in the Air Corps Reserve, so this was not unusual. Worth mentioning, however, is the fact that Lindbergh was also granted special permission to fly Navy aircraft. Since, from the Navy's point of view, Lindbergh was a private citizen, this was highly unusual, and, in fact, an unprecedented honor. *(Photo: Cradle of Aviation Museum.)*

211. Here Lindbergh is seen with famed humorist Will Rogers, around 1930. Rogers was to die in an air crash with aviator Wiley Post in 1935. *(Photo: Cradle of Aviation Museum.)*

208

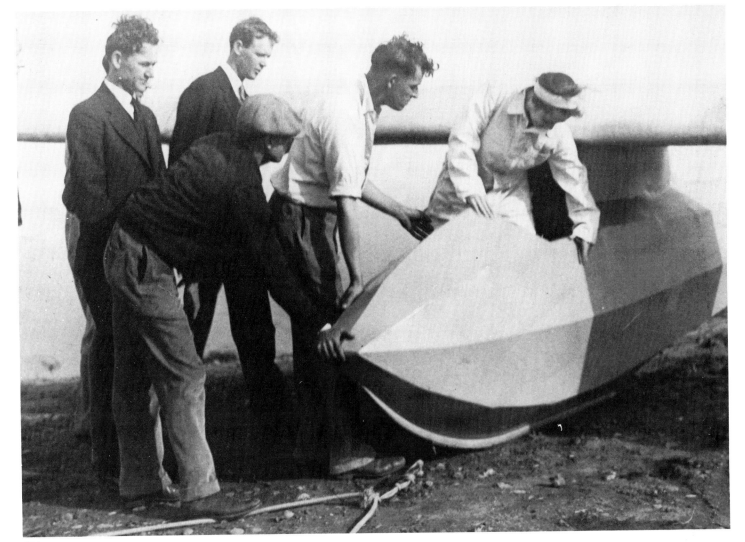

209

210

211

212

212. At the National Air Races in Cleveland in 1929, Lindbergh let Lockheed's Chief Engineer know that he was in the market for a fast new airplane for his personal use. The plane (which cost Lindbergh $22,825, a large sum in the Depression) was completed, after delays, in April 1930. Charles and Anne together flew this new plane, a Lockheed "Sirius," from California to New York on April 20, setting a new transcontinental speed record of 14 hours, 23 minutes. Anne by this time had learned navigation, and she contributed position finding to this, their first great flight together. The open cockpits made the flight a grueling one. On Anne's suggestion, they later had glass canopies installed. The plane's registration number was a restricted one, "NR-211," similar to that of the *Spirit of St. Louis*. *(Photos: Cradle of Aviation Museum.)*

213. Charles and Anne after they had arrived in New York with the new Lockheed Sirius. *(Photo: National Air and Space Museum.)*

213

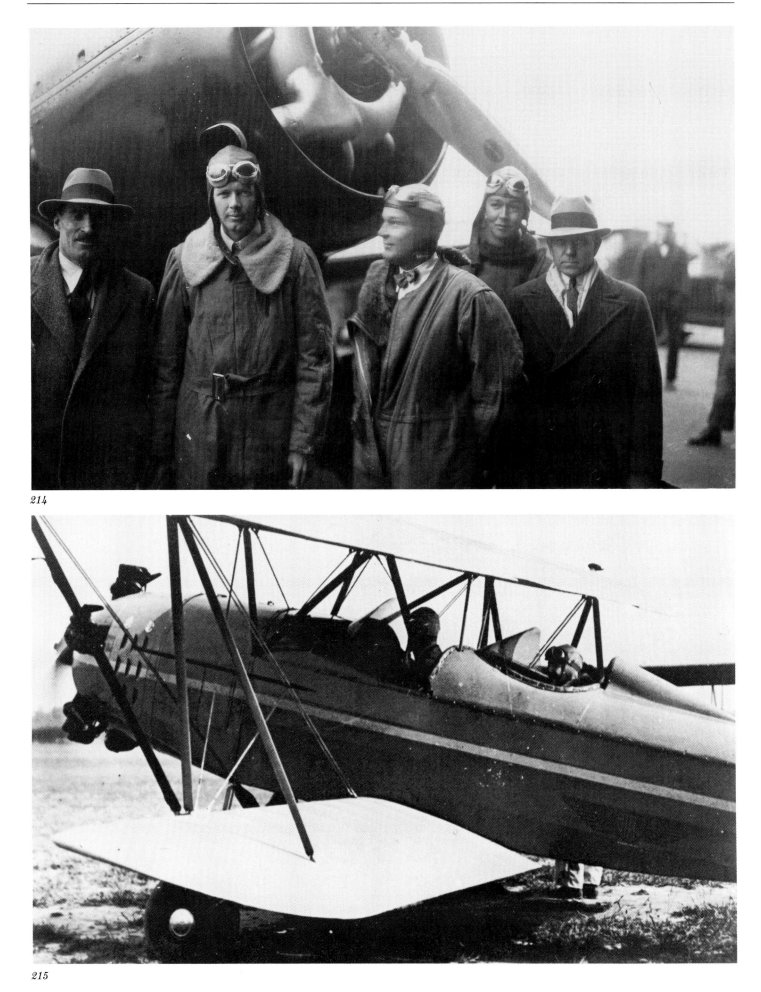

214

215

214. At Roosevelt Field with Casey Jones, left, the manager of the Curtiss Flying Service. The Lockheed Sirius had just (sometime in late 1930 or early 1931) had a new, more powerful engine installed, a 575-hp Wright Cyclone, in anticipation of a long survey flight that the Lindberghs were planning. *(Photo: National Air and Space Museum.)*

215, In 1931, Charles purchased a new Brunner-Winkle "Bird."
216. This was an excellent training plane, and with it, at the

Aviation Country Club in Hicksville, Long Island, he taught Anne to fly. Anne found her husband to be a strict, no-nonsense teacher. But she earned her license and became an efficient pilot. At the same time that she learned flying, Anne learned Morse Code and radio operation, to be among her major duties on the long survey flights the couple was to take in the years ahead. These two photos show the Lindberghs with the Bird. *(Photos: Robert Eisen Collection.)*

216

217

217. In order to help Juan Trippe, President of Pan American, survey new routes and landing sites, Lindbergh planned a long Great Circle flight to the Orient. Anne Morrow Lindbergh accompanied her husband on this rigorous journey, not as a mere passenger—she would only have been in the way—but, in his words, as "crew." Before starting out, Charles made sure that his wife had learned to fly the plane, as well as handle navigational and radio-operating duties. She proved to be an invaluable assistant to her husband in every way. This photograph shows them at the factory of the EDO Corporation, College Point, New York City, in mid-1931, where the two aluminum floats had just been installed. *(Photo: The EDO Corporation.)*

218

218. Photographers ogle the Lockheed, now on the ramp at the EDO factory, in 1931. Note that a sliding canopy has been installed (seen more clearly in the next photograph). The lines on the tail, called "drift lines," were used for judging wind speed and direction. This was without doubt the most advanced seaplane of its kind in the world at the time. *(Photo: The EDO Corporation.)*

219. Finally, on July 27, Charles and Anne took off from Flushing Bay in the Lockheed Sirius, beginning a journey that, by October, would carry them halfway around the world. As the flight was made in part to pioneer future air routes for Pan American Airways, Pan Am helped by providing logistical support in the form of radio stations and advance gasoline supplies at predetermined spots. The trip was also a welcome relief for the Lindberghs from all the intense media publicity. *(Photo: Cradle of Aviation Museum.)*

219

220

222

220. After leaving New York, the Lindberghs flew to North Haven, Maine, where they had arranged for their infant son to be left in the care of Anne's parents at their summer house. Here, vacationers in their small boats watch them as they prepare to depart. Charles and Anne may be seen toward the rear of the plane. *(Photo: Cradle of Aviation Museum.)*

221. The Lindberghs, on July 28, on their way to Ottawa, Canada, the next stop on their flight to the Orient. *(Photo: Cradle of Aviation Museum.)*

222. The Lockheed on the river near Ottawa. From here the next stop was Barrow, Alaska, then Nome. From there, they made an eleven-hour flight across the Bering Sea to Kamchatka in the Soviet Union. *(Photo: Cradle of Aviation Museum.)*

221

223

225

224

223. After Kamchatka they proceeded down the chain of Japanese islands, where bad weather caused them to make several forced landings. In this picture, Japanese sailors attempt to secure the plane in turbulent waters. *(Photo: National Air and Space Museum.)*

224. On August 26, the couple finally reached Tokyo, escorted by Japanese Navy planes. As always, they were honored in many receptions, at one of which they are shown here. *(Photo: Cradle of Aviation Museum.)*

225. In Osaka, on preparing to leave Japan, the Lindberghs found a stowaway crammed into the Lockheed's baggage compartment, seen at number "1" in this old news photo. Unaware that China would be the Lindberghs' actual next stop, the man had been hoping for a free ride to America. *(Photo: Cradle of Aviation Museum.)*

226. The Lindberghs then flew up the Yangtze River to Nanking, where they offered to use the Lockheed to assist famine-relief operations under way as a result of disastrous flooding. They engaged in aerial survey work, delivered medical supplies, then flew to Hangkow. At Hangkow, the British aircraft carrier *Hermes* became the base for the Sirius when it was too dangerous to anchor in the turbulent waters of the bay. Here the plane is being hoisted onto the ship. *(Photo: National Air and Space Museum.)*

227. The Lockheed Sirius on the deck of the *Hermes.* Unfortunately, on October 2, an accident that occurred while the plane was being lowered from the ship seriously damaged the plane

and cut short the Lindberghs' survey flight, which still had been the longest, most difficult flight yet undertaken by a seaplane, amounting to some ten thousand miles. The plane was shipped back to California for repair, and the Lindberghs returned to the states by ship. *(Photo: National Air and Space Museum.)*

228. This new Sikorsky S-40, a much larger flying boat than the S-38, was developed under Lindbergh's supervision, and he flew the first one to South America in 1931. Here the *American Clipper* is seen over New York. *(Photo: Cradle of Aviation Museum.)*

227

228

229

229. After the flight to the Far East, during the period of the hor-
rible affair of the kidnapping and murder of their child, the
Lockheed Sirius, back on wheels again, was used by
Lindbergh for various flights in the United States. In this
photo he is shown with his mother in front of the plane.
(Photo: Cradle of Aviation Museum.)

230. Lindbergh performing a stunt in a flying exhibition at an air
show in 1932. His plane is a pursuit Curtiss P-1B, a typical
Army Air Corps fighter of the day. *(Photo: National Air and
Space Museum.)*

231. On July 9, 1933, the Lindberghs departed from New York on
the second and final major survey flight in the Lockheed

Sirius, which had had a new engine installed and pontoons
refitted for the occasion. This flight was to be on the Great
Circle route to Europe by way of Labrador, Greenland and
Iceland. As with the previous flight, Pan American Airways
provided part of the support and was to receive some of the
benefits of their survey findings. Here, the Lindberghs are at
Hebron, Labrador, where they found the Eskimos friendly (as
they did elsewhere) but the mosquitoes extremely annoying.
The Lindberghs were forced to be self-sufficient at places like
this, where there were precious few amenities. They had
reached Hebron on July 21, and by July 25 they had flown to
Holsteinsborg, Greenland. *(Photo: National Air and Space
Museum.)*

230

231

232

233

234

232. The Sirius arrives at Holsteinsborg. This site, where they stayed until July 30, consisted essentially of a handful of colorful houses against a backdrop of rugged mountains. In the daytime they reconnoitered the area; at night they were the guests of the Governor. From here they made the dangerous crossing of the desolate, ice-covered interior of Greenland. They were well prepared for the worst, carrying with them a collapsible rubber sailboat, two complete radio sets, a sled, snowshoes, various items of hunting and camping equipment, eight gallons of water, and several weeks' worth of food. Anne maintained constant radio contact with the outside world for virtually the entire trip. *(Photo: National Air and Space Museum.)*

233. On August 6 the Lindberghs reached Angmagssalik, on the east coast of Greenland, a settlement notable only for its red houses on bleak hillsides against a backdrop of steep mountains. Here, an admiring Eskimo boy named the plane *Tingmissartoq,* Eskimo for "one who flies like a big bird." The Lindberghs liked this name and continued to use it. *(Photo: National Air and Space Museum.)*

234. In this photo taken in Greenland, Pan American's ship the *Jelling* may be seen at the left. This ship served as the Lindberghs' support base at several points of the journey. *(Photo: National Air and Space Museum.)*

236

237

235

235. The next stop was Reykjavik, Iceland, on August 15. After stops on the Faeroe and Shetland Islands, the Lindberghs arrived in Copenhagen, Denmark, on August 23. Here, members of the Royal Danish Navy, as well as some boats full of Danish youth, are seen meeting the plane. *(Photo: National Air and Space Museum.)*

236. After Copenhagen, the Lindberghs flew to several other European capitals. Here Anne's sister, Elizabeth, who had recently been married and was living in Europe, stands at the left (with flowers). *(Photo: Cradle of Aviation Museum.)*

237. A closeup of Anne Morrow Lindbergh in the rear cockpit of *Tingmissartoq*. She sometimes piloted the plane from this position when they were flying over open stretches where the limited visibility didn't matter. *(Photo: National Air and Space Museum.)*

238

239

238. When the Lindberghs visited Paris, *Tingmissartoq* was kept by courtesy of the French government at the Naval Seaplane base on the Seine River at Mureaux, where it is seen here, being hoisted from the river onto land. Lindbergh stands with his left leg on the left wing, while two sailors sit astride the tail to keep the plane balanced. *(Photo: National Air and Space Museum.)*

239. On November 11, en route to Lisbon, very bad weather forced the Lindberghs down on a small river separating Spain from Portugal. They stayed the night at Valença do Minho, a small town on the river. This photograph shows the Lindberghs with the citizens of Valença do Minho. The next day they flew to Lisbon, then the Azores, and finally Gambia, West Africa, where they would begin the return voyage, this time across the South Atlantic. They departed for South America on December 4, and, after encountering dangerous weather conditions on the sixteen-hour flight, arrived safely in Natal, Brazil. *(Photo: Cradle of Aviation Museum.)*

240. For several days the Lindberghs made their way north through South America and the Caribbean. On December 16, they finally departed Santo Domingo, in the Dominican Republic. Nine hours and 880 miles later, they arrived at Pan American's base near Miami, where this photograph shows them leaving *Tingmissartoq*. *(Photo: Cradle of Aviation Museum.)*

241. *Tingmissartoq* in flight. On December 19, the Lindberghs returned to the EDO seaplane base in New York. Their 30,000-mile survey flight reaped enormous benefits for Pan American. They had shown that adverse weather conditions were surmountable and radio aids workable. They had also returned with information on the suitability and unsuitability of numerous areas for future seaplane bases. The flight, unquestionably, was a triumph. *(Photo: Cradle of Aviation Museum.)*

241

240

242

242. *Tingmissartoq* at the American Museum of Natural History in New York, to which institution the Lindberghs presented the plane after their flight. In 1944, Lindbergh wrote in his diary: "It is now ten years that Tingmissartoq has been hanging silently in the Hall of the Ocean of Life, still trim and sleek and beautiful, a plane that was years ahead of its time. I stood looking at it, thinking of the places it had taken Anne and me, of the weather and the skies it had flown through, of the Arctic and the Tropic bays where it had landed, of the nights we slept together in that slender fuselage. . . ." Ultimately the plane was given to the Smithsonian Institution, where it hangs today (it is now in the Smithsonian's National Air and Space Museum), just yards from the *Spirit of St. Louis.* *(Photo: Glen Apfelbaum Collection.)*

243, In 1934 colorful entrepreneur, aircraft designer and pilot
244. Alexander de Seversky gave Lindbergh the opportunity to fly his Seversky SEV-3, the fastest amphibian of its day. The sleek, bronze-colored SEV-3 was similar in lines to the Lockheed Sirius that Lindbergh had flown from 1930 to 1933, and no doubt he enjoyed flying it. In the first of these two photos, Seversky shows Lindbergh the SEV-3's controls, and in the second Lindbergh is seated in the cockpit. The setting is North Beach Airport, on the site of what is now La Guardia Airport in New York City. *(Photos: Cradle of Aviation Museum.)*

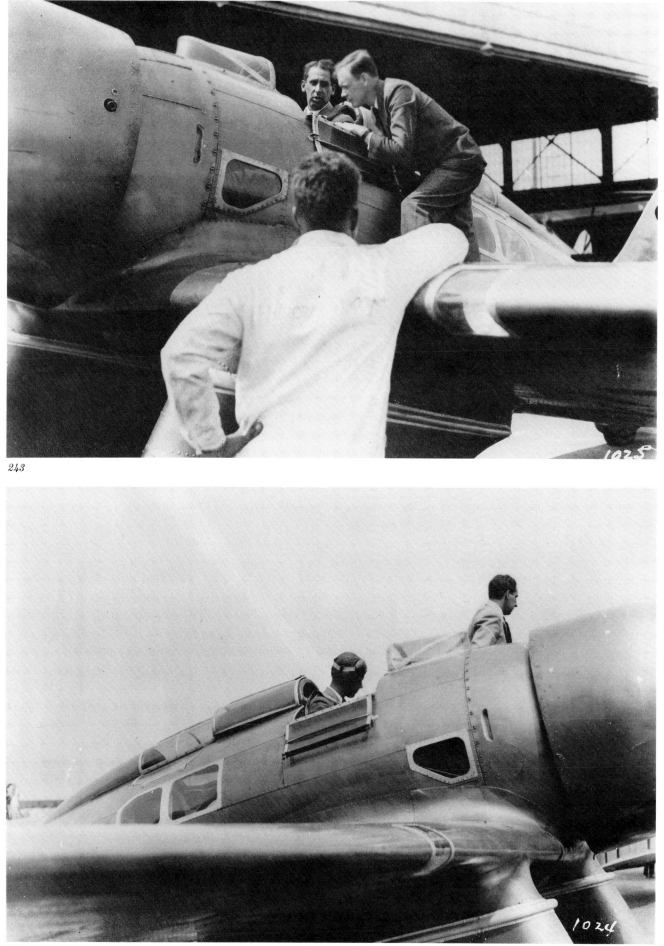

243

244

245

246

247

245. Lindbergh became close friends with pioneer aircraft designer Igor Sikorsky, with whom he collaborated on the design of the new flying boats being inaugurated in transoceanic service. Here the two men are seen with the latest model in 1934, the S-42. *(Photo: United Technologies Corp.)*

246. The kidnapping and murder of Charles Jr. was a severe shock from which the Lindberghs never completely recovered, even after the culprit, Bruno Richard Hauptmann, had been tried, convicted and executed. Here Lindbergh can be seen entering the courtroom during the Hauptmann trial at the end of 1934. *(Photo: Cradle of Aviation Museum.)*

247. When TWA (TAT became TWA in October 1930) was looking for a new airliner to replace their old Tri-Motors, Lindbergh persuaded them to require Douglas to design a twin-engine plane that could execute single-engine takeoffs with a full load from any airport on TWA's routes. This was an important influence on the aircraft designs in progress at Douglas, and the result, eventually, was the famous DC-3 (seen here), first flown in 1935. Thus Lindbergh played a part in the development of one of the safest, best-designed airplanes ever built. *(Photo: Cradle of Aviation Museum.)*

248

250

249

248. Robert Goddard, the pioneer of rocket technology, was considered a crackpot when he started his experiments in the mid-1920's. In late 1929, Carol Guggenheim (Harry's wife) showed her husband and Lindbergh an article about this obscure experimenter. Intrigued, Lindbergh visited Goddard. Lindbergh's superior scientific understanding of flight enabled him to comprehend the importance of Goddard's work, and he persuaded Harry and his father Daniel Guggenheim (founder of the Guggenheim Fund), as well as the Carnegie Institution, to award Goddard enough money to carry on his experiments. Thus Lindbergh was instrumental in supporting the pioneering experimentation in rocket-powered flight that would one day put men on the moon. In this 1935 photograph Goddard stands between Harry Guggenheim and Lindbergh. *(Photo: National Air and Space Museum.)*

249. Another view of Goddard, at work on one of his rockets.

250. Weary of all the publicity and the constant interference of the press in their lives, wishing to escape unpleasant memories, and concerned about the safety of their son Jon, who had been born on August 16, 1932, the Lindberghs, after Hauptmann's execution in 1936, finally decided to move to Europe, where they remained for some years. Although they were left alone while living in the English countryside, whenever they went into large cities they felt the need to travel incognito. Here they stroll through the streets of Paris. *(Photo: Cradle of Aviation Museum.)*

251. Charles Lindbergh, being who he was, could hardly do without an airplane of his own for very long. As soon as he arrived in England for an extended stay, he ordered a custom-built Miles "Mohawk," seen in this photo. This sporty little plane carried him and Anne throughout Europe and even as far as India. *(Photo: National Air and Space Museum.)*

251

252

253

254

252. Charles had always had an interest in Eastern mysticism, philosophies and religions, and Anne, as a writer, was curious about all sorts of things. Therefore the Lindberghs flew their Mohawk to the Middle East and then to India, where they attended the World Parliament of Religions. The flight was described by Anne in her book *The Steep Ascent*, which gives a gripping account of the dangers encountered while crossing the fog-covered Alps. Here, at Bombay Aerodrome, Charles assists famed British explorer Sir Francis Younghusband into the Mohawk before flying to Calcutta. *(Photo: Cradle of Aviation Museum.)*

253. Lindbergh with an unknown person standing in front of a Curtiss P-36 fighter belonging to the 33rd Pursuit Squadron, 1938. *(Photo: National Air and Space Museum.)*

254. In the late 1930's, Lindbergh visited the military aviation facilities of a number of European countries, reporting on them dutifully to the American government. By far the most controversial of these visits were those made to Germany. Lindbergh was accused of being a Nazi sympathizer, yet the visits were made at the request of Maj. Truman Smith, U.S. military attaché in Berlin, and Lindbergh kept nothing he learned about German air power a secret from the U.S. government. Here, the Lindberghs are seen at Tempelhof Field, Berlin, on October 11, 1938, where they attended an International Air Congress. *(Photo: Cradle of Aviation Museum.)*

255. Lindbergh inspecting German air facilities. Maj. Truman Smith is at right. *(Photo: Cradle of Aviation Museum.)*

255

256

256. In Germany Lindbergh had a glimpse of the frightening size to which German air power had grown. Here he was photographed at a formal affair with Gen. Erhard Milch, second in charge of the Luftwaffe. *(Photo: Cradle of Aviation Museum.)*

257. When the United States entered World War II, Lindbergh felt that his noninterventionist, isolationist views were no longer appropriate, and he wanted to participate in the fighting. Nevertheless, his old views were held against him and he was unable to regain his old Air Corps commission. For a while he was able to serve his country by working as a consultant to Henry Ford, helping produce B-24 bombers at Ford's Willow Run plant (seen here). *(Photo: Cradle of Aviation Museum.)*

258. After his work at the Ford plant, Lindbergh became a consultant to the United Aircraft Corporation, devoting his time to helping make the Chance-Vought Division's F4U "Corsair" a combat-worthy fighter. In April 1944 he traveled to the Pacific, ostensibly as a civilian adviser to the Navy and Army Air Forces. In reality, he participated in combat, demonstrating the potential of the Corsair by being the first to fly it with a 4,000-pound bomb load on actual strike missions. A Corsair with a bomb attached is seen here at a Pacific base. *(Photo: Cradle of Aviation Museum.)*

259. Another military plane of advanced design that Lindbergh had a chance to fly was the Lockheed P-38 "Lightning," shown here. What may have been his most important contribution to the war effort came when he used his flying expertise and experience to teach Army pilots methods of fuel conservation, enabling them to keep the P-38 aloft for ten hours without refueling, whereas, flown the usual way, it could last in the air only seven. *(Photo: Cradle of Aviation Museum.)*

257

258

259

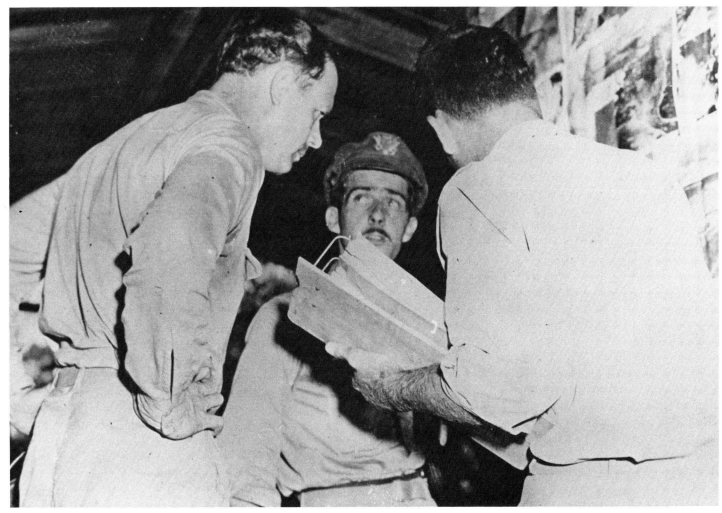

260

260. Although he was 42 years old, Lindbergh participated in fifty combat missions in the Pacific. He bombed Japanese targets, shot down one "Zero" and was nearly shot down himself. Here he confers with noted ace Maj. Thomas McGuire at Biak Island (off New Guinea) in June 1944. *(Photo: Glen Apfelbaum Collection.)*

261. After the war was over in Europe, in May 1945, Lindbergh was invited to join a Naval technical mission to Germany to investigate new developments in jets and rockets. On arrival, Lindbergh was shocked when he saw the damage our bombing had done to German cities, as well as the horrors of German concentration camps. After touring German rocket-production facilities and interviewing a number of German aeronautical experts, however, Lindbergh came away

impressed by the V-2 and other developments in German rocketry. On his return from overseas, he urged broad development along the same lines in the United States. To facilitate this, captured V-2's were transported to this country after the war. The one in this photo is being tested at White Sands, New Mexico. *(Photo: U.S. Air Force.)*

262. After the war, Lindbergh continued as a consultant to the military. At one point, Gen. Carl Spaatz, Chief of the Air Force, asked him to serve as a special R and D consultant. This was the kind of role Lindbergh enjoyed, and he granted these requests with pleasure. Here he inspects a new Navy "drone" (pilotless plane) in Philadelphia, June 1947. Gen. Jimmy Doolittle, in civilian clothes, is at right. *(Photo: Cradle of Aviation Museum.)*

261

262

263. In the 1950's, Lindbergh was a member of the Air Force science advisory board, working with the distinguished mathematician and physicist John von Neumann and with scientist H. Guyford Stever on the development of nuclear weapons and ballistic missiles. As he studied these matters, he became an enthusiastic advocate of ICBM's, such as the *Atlas* missile seen here. In 1954, in recognition of his defense work, President Eisenhower finally restored Lindbergh's Air Force Reserve commission and promoted him to brigadier general. *(Photo: General Dynamics Corp.)*

264. Lindbergh's best-selling, Pulitzer-Prize-winning book *The Spirit of St. Louis* (1953) led in 1957 to a feature film of the same name, starring James Stewart. During the course of filming, which took place partly in California and partly on Long Island, the real Lindbergh flew the replica *Spirit* for an hour. Here Stewart, as a twenty-five-year-old Lindbergh, is seen at the Ryan plant inspecting the periscope to be installed in the *Spirit*. *(Photo: Cradle of Aviation Museum.)*

265. After World War II, Lindbergh was also in demand as a civil-aeronautics consultant, particularly to Pan American Airways, which he had supported from its inception in 1929. In his consultant's role he played a leading part in the approval and development of all types of aircraft newly considered or adopted by Pan American, including America's first commercial jet airliner, the revolutionary Boeing 707, seen here. *(Photo: Cradle of Aviation Museum.)*

263

264

265

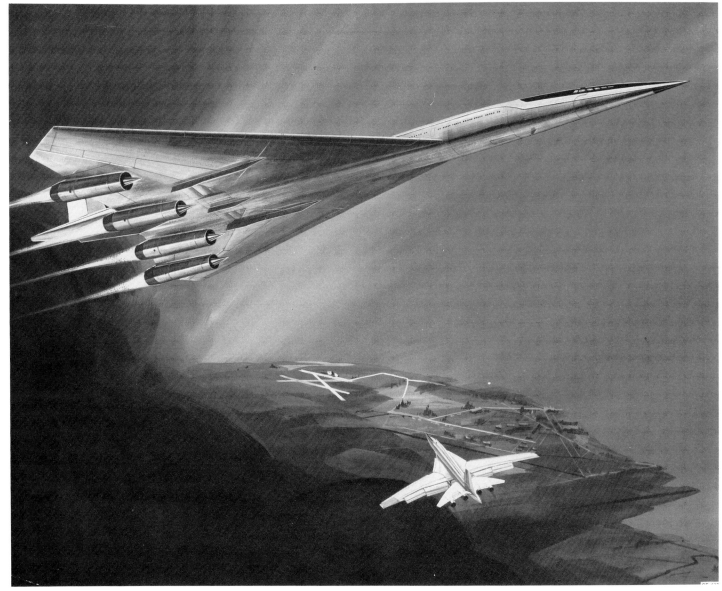

266

266. Although he was as fully steeped as anyone in the world of airplane technology, Lindbergh never blindly accepted exotic new developments. When it appeared that the proposed American SST would be extremely costly to develop and operate and would have a harmful effect on the environment, Lindbergh became an outspoken opponent. He persuaded Pan Am to abandon its intent to invest in the SST, and this was a fatal blow to the project. This photo from the 1960's shows an artist's conception of the SST. *(Photo: The Boeing Company.)*

267

267. Although a fervent supporter of Robert Goddard's rocket experiments as far back as 1929, Lindbergh never got to witness any of Goddard's important launchings. Forty years later, he did, however, witness one of the most amazing launchings of them all: that of the *Apollo* spacecraft that put two astronauts on the moon. In this photograph taken at Cape Kennedy on July 15, 1969, the day before liftoff, Lindbergh chats with the man whose company had built the *Spirit of St. Louis* for him, Claude Ryan. He also had an opportunity to meet the astronauts, who were about to embark on a voyage of discovery analogous to the one he had made himself 42 years before. *(Photo: Cradle of Aviation Museum.)*

268. Launching of the *Apollo 11* on July 16, 1969. After viewing this scene, Lindbergh wrote that he was "hypnotized by the launching," whose "billowing, flashing chaos shook with the Earth itself. For a moment, reality and memory contorted, and Robert Goddard stood watching at my side. Was he now the dream; his dream the reality?" *(Photo: Cradle of Aviation Museum.)*

268

269

269. In the fall of 1973, past and present met for Charles Lindbergh in an unlikely location: the basement of the Long Island home of George Dade (at right in the photo), who as a teenager had helped him adjust a parachute at Curtiss Field 45 years earlier (see photo 188). Members of the Long Island Early Fliers Club were in the process of restoring Lindbergh's original Curtiss "Jenny" (see photos 8–12), which they had retrieved from an Iowa farmer. Lindbergh was able to verify that the plane was indeed the one he had flown in his barnstorming days. The Jenny is now on exhibit at Long Island's Cradle of Aviation Museum (of which Dade was the Founding Director) at Mitchel Field in Garden City, New York. *(Photo: Cradle of Aviation Museum.)*

270. A portrait of a pensive Charles Lindbergh near the end of his life. The last decade of his life was devoted in large part to aiding environmental and humanitarian causes. He also worked on autobiographical writings, including his *Wartime Journals*, published in 1970, and the posthumously published *Autobiography of Values*. In 1972 he learned he had lymphoma, which, although his case was originally thought treatable, in less than two years turned into a more serious form of the cancer and killed him. *(Photo: National Air and Space Museum.)*

270

271

271. Knowing that he had such a short time left, Lindbergh, against the advice of his doctors, discharged himself from Columbia-Presbyterian Hospital in New York and spent his last days with Anne at his favorite home in Maui, where he planned his funeral and burial as carefully as he had planned his long-distance flights. With Anne at his side, Charles Lindbergh died peacefully on the morning of August 26, 1974. On his grave stone (seen here) is inscribed a simple selection he chose from the 139th Psalm: "... If I take the wings of the morning, and dwell in the uttermost parts of the sea ..." *(Photo: Robert F. Eisen.)*

272. Lindbergh's grave site on Maui as it appeared in the early 1990's. *(Photo: Robert F. Eisen.)*

272

Index

NOTE: Roman numerals indicate *pages*; Arabic numerals indicate *captions*.